SHIPPING CONTAINER HOMES FOR BEGINNERS

The Complete Step-By-Step Guide to Building Your Affordable, Eco-Friendly, and Super-Cozy Container Home from Scratch | BONUS: Floor Plans and Design Ideas

ADAM SALNER

TABLE OF CONTENTS

INTRODUCTION

I am living in a home made of steel. This sentence sounds bizarre and untrue, right? But unlike the man of steel, this home of steel is not a fantasy but a reality. Yes, you heard it right, people are getting familiar with these steel houses as the world is discovering innovative pathways for increasing living standards. Building a home using containers is not fiction anymore.

If you have ever wondered what the word "shipping container home" means, then you're in the right place. Most people have heard these words many times, but they have no idea what they are. A shipping container home is exactly what it sounds like. Since a shipping container is a home for things that need transportation, then shipping container homes are homes for humans. As the world is advancing towards innovation and technology, the world is getting more familiar with the idea of shipping container homes. Though at first glance you will not quite get what you would expect in a normal home, as you explore and look at the characteristics, you will get to know the amazing advantages that they have. All in all, it is unfair to say that a shipping container home is not the right place to invest in.

These homes are economical and eco-friendly. Both of these things are the demand of the future, and, in no time, we will see these container homes everywhere. They are the face of the future, albeit a bit different from what people may have thought. A shipping container home is made of recycled shipping containers, just like the ones that you see in movies. Storage containers and cargo containers are mostly used to build shipping container homes. Shipping container homes come in two different sizes; the first is 20 feet by 8 feet and the second is 40 feet by 8 feet. You can opt for whichever you want or whichever suits your budget. Depending on your need, the home can be one container or a combination of multiple containers.

Now that you are familiar with shipping container homes, we will dive into the details. The first-ever shipping container was made back in 1956. Not in his wildest dream did Malcolm McLean think that one day people would be living in one of these. Shipping container homes are your doorway to being an eco-friendly human being while saving a lot of money. This book will be a step-by-step guide for all those who wish to build shipping container homes for themselves. I will also be adding the case study of Todd and Di Miller's container home that gained attention and started the trend of container homes.

Whether you want to build a home for yourself or you want to invest in a container home, you will be provided with all the information here. From the price of one container to the overall budget and the best procedure for building a cyclone-proof container home, we will cover everything. This book will be your ultimate guide for container homes, and after finishing it, I guarantee that you will be adamant to invest your money in this budget-friendly and eco-friendly home. Trust me, building your own container home is not an impossible mission at all!

CHAPTER 1:

History of Shipping Container

I f you think that the trend of shipping container homes started just around this year, then let me correct you. Enthusiasts are divided on the history and foundations of the first-ever shipping containers. Some say that it was back in 1987 when a man named Philip Clark made his and the world's first-ever shipping container home, however, this didn't spark a trend among others. Other people believe that the first-ever shipping container home was built back in 2007. Yes, that is exactly 14 years ago. An architect from California, whose name is Peter DeMaria, created the first-ever shipping container home.

Todd And di Miller's Shipping Home Container

Shipping container homes did not gain in popularity until after 2012. This was the year when an Australian couple named Todd and Di Miller lost their home in a heavy flood. Despite the grief and heavy loss, the couple didn't lose their willpower and decided to build themselves a new home. Now, we all know how costly it can be to build a home in countries like Australia from scratch. But the couple were very sharp, and they used their brains to create something so exquisite yet so affordable. Yes, building your own container home is not a dream anymore, so unleash your inner builder and architect.

They created a six thousand square foot mansion out of thirty-one containers. The couple also gave a name to their container home. After the Graceville Container Home was featured on an Australian TV channel, people started to talk about this innovative new home and it eventually gained popularity.

Their six thousand square foot, four-bedroom home was built from thirty-one shipping containers. That's right, thirty-one! Flood-proofing was a priority in the design of the new house. There would be ten shipping containers on the ground floor that would be used as garages, gyms, offices, pools, and art studios. There would be eleven containers stacked on top of each other and a huge open-plan living room that included a kitchen, bathroom, study, and three bedrooms. Ten more containers were used to build the third floor, which contains a master bedroom, walk-in closet, bathroom, and terrace area. In total, US $310,000 was spent on a swimming pool, art studio, gym, and four bedrooms.

Basis Of the Home

Purchasing the containers was their first task. The couple agreed to purchase the containers from China. One container cost them $2,900. Detailed exterior and interior painting, proper welding, and a 28 mm thick plywood floor completed the design of the containers. In preparation for the construction of their new home, they demolished their old one and laid foundations. As part of the foundation, Todd drilled micropiles nine meters deep and grouted them into the surrounding soil to 'glue' them together. These kinds of foundations are cyclone-proof. On top of the piles were concrete piers on which steel containers were placed. Clearing the site and completing the foundation took about a month.

Todd ordered the first ten containers shortly thereafter. Concrete piers were laid down on top of each container after it was lifted into place. They finished welding the containers together within four hours of the ground floor being completed. Several more containers were delivered two weeks later, which were used to construct their first floor. The next step was to place the containers on top of the ground. After placing them firmly on top of it, they were welded together. In the next two weeks, the final ten containers were shipped to their site. A crane was used to place the containers on top of one another.

Designing

Taking the steel containers apart and reshaping them into a house was the next step. The containers' opening was reinforced with thick universal steel beams to maintain their integrity. To allow hot air to escape during the summer, they used tinted Low-E glass for the windows. After fixing the first container in place, it took eight weeks for the building to become watertight. Rock wool insulation sheets were used to insulate the walls of the second and third stories, and wooden frames were used to hold them in place. A concrete-colored render was plastered over the walls once the insulation had been completed. To highlight the steel, Di decided to keep the ceilings exposed.

A coat of paint was then applied to the house. The interior of the box was painted with three layers of white Dulux wash and wear paint. Dulux infra cool was applied in eight layers externally. In addition, the paint used prevents UV rays from entering the house and deflects some of the heat. The bamboo flooring in the house was installed after the paint had dried. They used up-cycled materials throughout the house including timber, railway sleepers, glass, and Tasmanian oak as part of their eco-conscious design. There is even an underground system that collects greywater and flushes the toilets with it.

The Final Look

It took them until July 2013 to finish their home and move in. A lifetime guarantee is offered by the engineers of the house. Additionally, it was built according to Queensland's latest flood-prone building regulations and is cyclone proof. The container home is the largest ever built in Australia.

The home was built in 24 weeks for $450,000 in total. Due to several design changes made during construction, it cost more than expected. But you can build yours at a cheaper price and invest in an affordable container home. An additional bathroom and a swimming pool that weren't part of the original plan were added. They also spent $40,000 on landscaping. When they sold it for over $1,090,000 at the end of 2014, they proved their extra expense was worth it.

CHAPTER 2:

Should I Buy Used Containers?

For The US Market

Buying a used container comes with a lot of risks in itself. Many countries and states deal specifically in selling these used containers to their clients. People in the American market buy used containers because of their low cost and many other advantages. Listed below are a few advantages of buying used containers in the USA.

Cost-Effective

Buying used shipping containers offers several obvious benefits, including their low price and affordability. It is possible to buy a new shipping container for as little as $2,000 or as much as $10,000. In contrast, you can expect to pay between $800 and about $3,000 for a used shipping container. Although the cost will vary depending on where you purchase your used container, it will always be cheaper than a new container. The portable nature of these products allows you to move them without spending a ton of money. However, if you plan to transport it across the country, acquiring a shipping container can incur a significant cost. New containers can be built and sent by container shipping companies rather quickly, so time isn't wasted. On average, it takes more than three months to receive new shipping containers from overseas. Used containers are hard to find, but they can be found in most areas if you know where to look.

Eco-Friendly

The environmental benefits of buying used as opposed to new containers are also worth noting. With used shipping containers, the manufacturing of new containers is slowed down, reducing the emission of dangerous greenhouse gases. The reduction of steel waste is another benefit because by buying used containers you do not waste steel.

Durability

Containers designed for shipping are long-lasting and incredibly durable. Traditionally, they are kept outdoors most of the time and can withstand any weather condition. A lot of weight can be placed on them, so there is little chance of earthquakes destroying them. Because steel is capable of both cooling and heating, its temperature is a bit tricky to control. However, the inside environment will not be affected by varying temperatures if the building is well insulated. It is important to note that rust can form inside shipping containers, and the outside location accelerates the process, so it is necessary to take good care of shipping containers and to make sure they are maintained properly.

The Disadvantages of Buying a Used Container

However, there is a disadvantage that you must consider when thinking of buying a used container. Used containers for home purposes are not the most suitable and wisest choice. Why? Because used containers may be more damaged compared to new containers. Building your permanent home on something that has low strength can be a hazard and a red flag that you must consider. You must look at the condition of the container before making a final decision about purchasing it. You cannot risk your life and the lives of your loved ones, so make sure that the container is in good condition before making any decisions.

Breakdown Of the Cost

Here is the breakdown of the cost when you are using a used shipping container or a brand-new shipping container to build your container home. This is a rough estimate, and the prices can vary according to your state and the current prices. The used shipping container costs around $2500. If you are using a brand-new container, then it can cost up to $4500 to $5000. The windows cost around $3200. You must remember that if you are living in a place where there is a chance of hurricanes and tornadoes, then you need laminated glass windows and the prices of that can vary. The insulation boards can cost up to $1000. For the metal framing, you need $700. For electrical purposes, you need $1500. Plumbing requires $1800, whereas, for drywall, you need $720. Flooring can cost up to $750. The heating and cooling system can go up to $900. For the kitchen you need cabinets, and they can cost up to $2200. Countertops can go for over $700, mill work is around $600, and the cost of paint can be over $250.

You must know that this is still a rough idea, and, as stated above, you must always have more than the amount needed – new problems can pop up at the last moment and you might need to spend money on something extra that is necessary for building your shipping container home.

CHAPTER 3:

Investing in a
Shipping Container Home

If you have made up your mind to invest in a shipping container home, there are a few things that you need to think about. You will enjoy many benefits of living in a container home, but the most important thing to do right now is to decide your budget. How much money you can invest is the real question and everything else comes after that.

Decide Your Budget

If you have no clue about budgeting for a container home, then taking advice from property dealers or related agencies can help you a lot. Once your budget is determined, you can proceed with other things. The next thing you need to do is find all the right materials that are within your budget. You can search online stores or visit different physical shops (whichever is most convenient).

If you are not comfortable with a forty-foot container, my suggestion is that you go with a twenty-foot container. It is not an obligation that you must have a forty-foot container if it exceeds your budget. Whether you are looking for a single-family home or multi-family, my goal is to find the right fit for you and not to push you into something that is beyond what you can afford. That is why I will advise you to look at different online websites to see different sizes of containers. Once you see the different prices of containers, it will be easier for you to determine the best price and size for you.

Most people like to personalize their container home with some upgrades and maybe even a custom feature or two. When looking at the price, please allow for these in your budget. You're halfway there once you select the floor plan. To get a good idea of your overall cost, you should consider the land price (if you do not own it) and the preparation costs including foundations, utilities, driveways, etc. An experienced general contractor can give you a ballpark figure. You can ask the seller of these containers to provide the contractor with the preliminary information for a ballpark price.

For The US Market

Now that you have a rough idea of how much it costs for a container home, you need a few more details to see where you stand and how much you need to loan. First things first, you need to sit back and think about how big you want your new house to be. Do you need a small two-bedroom kind of apartment or is there a luxury dining room with a swimming pool and a couple of extra bedrooms involved? You cannot apply for a loan without knowing the exact size of the house that you need.

Whether or not you can afford a shipping container home will be answered here. By looking at the case study of Todd and Di Miller, you might have realized that some container comes can be quite pricey. But they are pricey because of all the additional rooms and luxuries that can be added. You can opt for a small single-story two-bedroom kind of apartment, which will be a lot cheaper, so don't be disheartened.

Write Down Your Budget

You can get a cost estimate based on an educated guess of how much you should expect to pay. It represents a plan for how finite resources will be allocated to pay those expenses. The critical thing to remember is that both can be based on data from the present or the future. It's a fact that what you want or can afford today is not necessarily what you will want or be able to afford next year. Therefore, incorporating both of these ideas can help you to set goals when designing your life, not just your home.

Cost estimates and budgets are closely linked, and you cannot have a successful project without both. If you want to know whether a shipping container home is right for you or what you can afford, you need to know how much the different types of shipping container homes cost. Writing down your budget not only involves the cost of the containers but also the furniture inside them. For instance, the average price of the furniture in a bedroom in the US costs around $2050. You need to double the price if there are going to be two rooms. You have to do the same with the kitchen, bathroom, living room, your front yard, etc.

Background Information

Estimation is more of an art than a science, and this makes it important to know. It is common for two people to use similar estimating techniques but still produce slightly different estimates when given the same constraints. It is because there is a wide range of products that can be used and all of them vary in terms of cost. An estimate will always be variable in part because of unknowns, which require some judgment calls and lead to uncertainty.

There is no magic involved in estimating. Based on imperfect and limited information, it is the process of predicting and guessing. However, as time goes on, you'll gather more information about your specific project, so you'll be able to produce a more accurate estimate as you go along. An expert estimator can prepare a cost estimate for you, but they will need specific plans and specifications to work from. Many people make most of their decisions on the spot and have a lot of ideas stored in their heads. Due to this, even without considering the costs associated with a shipping container home, a professional cost estimate would be impractical, and you would be best advised to create your estimate.

It is important to have clarity about what you want to estimate before you create an estimate for yourself. The project scope includes, obviously, the site's location. However, whether you intend to hire a contractor or do it yourself is just as important. It is the same procedure regardless of how you do it. In addition to profit and overheads, there are other factors to consider when estimating the cost of a contractor. It is always a good idea to add a few more dollars to your final amount.

Know the Blind Spots

The ability to know how much you don't know is often said to be a good indicator of personal maturity. When you are humble enough to recognize the gaps in your knowledge, you will proceed with greater caution and find ways to strengthen your weaknesses. This principle is equally informative when it comes to cost estimation. Wrong or incomplete estimates can have a serious impact on the accuracy of your plans. Because of this, it's crucial to do a little inventory of what you know and don't know. These are the familiar facts you know and are aware of. You must have these facts in mind before making a final budget because sometimes there are things that you do not see at first, but they turn out to be crucial later on.

Knowing the unknown represents the knowledge you might not be aware of personally, but that you have when dealing with someone you trust or when using resources you have available to you. A government office, a local contractor, or information from Discover Containers can all provide useful insight. Including this information in your estimate is straightforward. Identified risks are the unknowable-knowns: this is where things can get tricky. The costs exist and you agree they should be included in your estimate, but nobody can reliably quantify them. Even though the exact risk cannot be predicted, it can be evaluated with judgment and probability. It is reasonable to estimate that you will be able to complete the work with the machine within two days. However, because you haven't worked with the machine before, you can estimate that you will rent it for three days just to be on the safe side.

Unknowable-unknowns should also be taken into consideration. Complete ignorance is when you do not even realize that such an unknown exists, let alone attempt to account for it accurately. Oftentimes, such expenditures are not anticipated and are not even considered because they are so unforeseen or unexpected. A great example of this is the COVID-19 pandemic of 2020. If you need to estimate these costs, you should include a contingency line item. There should be enough contingency funds to deal with one of these scenarios in the event that it occurs.

CHAPTER 4:

Three Options
for Container Homes

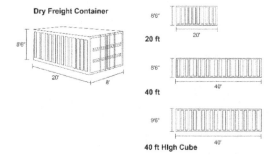

Dry Freight Container

20 ft

40 ft

40 ft High Cube

Building It Yourself

A lot of people wonder whether they can build the container home themselves. Well, you can build it with your own blood, sweat, and tears. You can use all of your designs and creativity alongside your practical skills while making your DIY container home. However, there are some drawbacks worth considering. Below are the advantages and disadvantages of building a container home yourself.

Advantages of Building a Shipping Container Home by Yourself

Your shipping container home will be cheaper if you build it yourself. Doing most or all of the labor yourself saves you a ton of money over paying someone else. Making it yourself also guarantees that it will be built correctly and that shortcuts will be avoided. Your builder won't rush the insulation and roofing because they are running out of time, so you know that these jobs will be done correctly. Additionally, the container home can be styled and designed in any way you want since you are designing and building it yourself. How about stacking the containers on top of each other? That depends on whether you make it yourself!

In addition, if your opinion changes halfway through the home building process, then you are free to change the design (although you are not recommended to make significant changes in midstream). In this case, it is more difficult and sometimes impossible to change the design of the prefabricated container home or the contractor's plan.

Disadvantages of Building a Shipping Container Home by Yourself

Not having the right skills, experience, and knowledge is one of the biggest obstacles during the construction process. It is recommended that you have some DIY experience, but you do not have to have built a container home before. Additionally, if you already have a full-time job or must continue to fulfill other time-consuming responsibilities, getting started on such a project can be particularly challenging. The process of building a container home is just as time-consuming and difficult as building any other house. Having a job does not make it impossible to do what you need to do, it just makes it a little harder to juggle everything. Despite the hard work that goes into building a home, some people have done it. Keep an open mind and understand that since you are employed, it will take longer to finish than it would otherwise.

Hiring a Contractor

For many people, the best option is to hire a contractor as they cannot give their full time to the home building themselves. This is a good option, but again, it has its pros and cons.

Advantages of Hiring a Contractor

Choosing a contractor has the biggest benefit of giving you access to their experience and expertise. You should not be surprised that these individuals take their jobs seriously and tend to guarantee their work because they live and breathe construction. Hiring a contractor also has the advantage of saving you time. It would be much faster if five or six people were working on your container home simultaneously rather than just you. When you also work full-time, you may only have time to work on your home on weekends and evenings. The majority of your container home can be built by you, but you can hire a contractor to do the welding.

Disadvantages of Hiring a Contractor

Hiring a contractor has two major disadvantages. Both of these disadvantages are very true for most people as they cannot afford to spend much money. The first thing to consider is the cost. You may have to hire contractors to do your work because it is much more expensive than doing the work yourself. During the construction of container homes, hiring a contractor might be the biggest expense.

Although they are experienced, they can charge you heavily. You should understand that it is not their fault because they earn money through this job. However, considering you just spent a lot of money on buying and shipping the containers, taking out money for a contractor can be hard. In addition, finding a reputable and experienced contractor can take a lot of your time, which you may not be able to waste. All that being said, having a good contractor on your side is invaluable, especially if problems arise.

Prefabricated Shipping Containers

Buying ready-made container homes is another option. This type of ready-made shipping container home comes with both advantages and disadvantages. It's not uncommon for prefab container homes to be sold as empty shells that are ready to be moved into immediately. People also refer to it as a turnkey home. They vary between models and manufacturers in terms of specifications and interior design. For people who are either too busy or have inadequate expertise to build a shipping container home, prefabricated homes are a wonderful alternative. Also, you can use them if you lack the necessary space, equipment, or facilities to convert your containers on site.

Advantages of Prefabricated Container Homes

It is certainly true that the major advantage of prefab homes is that they can be built so quickly. Almost no research is necessary, but there is still some planning and design involved. Stocks are generally kept on hand by prefab companies. Container homes are already built and only need to be shipped to you, placed on foundation blocks, and set up with utilities. The peace of mind that comes with buying a prefabricated home is another benefit. Whether you do it yourself or hire a contractor, building your own house can be stressful at times. Prefabricated homes may be a good option for people who need to avoid extra stress in their lives. Because you will know exactly how your home will look when it's finished, a prefabricated home reduces the anxiety about the unknown. Additionally, prefab companies often help with permitting and planning.

Disadvantages of Prefabricated Container Homes

A prefabricated home has the largest disadvantage of "what you see is what you get". Containers are generally non-customizable, meaning that the only models available to you are those offered by the company. Prefab homes are costly, which is the second disadvantage. Prefabricated container homes are always more expensive than all the other options discussed in this article. A developer oversees the entire build for you, so you're paying them for their services. Many people build a container home to save money, not to spend more. While some people will not necessarily have an issue with this, others will. You are the only one who can make this decision, so choose wisely.

CHAPTER 5:

What You Need When Building Shipping Container Homes by Yourself

I f you have decided to build the container home yourself, then here is a list of the most important things that you need. Make sure you have the best equipment (and manpower) so that you don't have to struggle to complete the job.

Welder

You need a welder for a lot of things when building a container home. Here are a few of the tasks that you need a welder for:

- Welding the containers of the foundation pads
- Welding the containers together in case you want to make a double-story house
- Welding the doors and windows
- Welding other supports of the container

Welders, which are best used in container homes, are among the most common topics of discussion among enthusiasts. The following are some of the most popular options:

1. SMAW (Shielded Metal Arc Welding)

- Consumable electrodes are used with a stick welder
- A continuous electrode is formed by a spool of flux-core wire in a wire-feed welder

2. GMAW (Gas Metal Arc Welding)

- The MIG (Metal Inert Gas) welding process uses a wire spool as a continuous electrode in conjunction with shielding gas supplied externally

3. GTAW (Welding with Tungsten Gas Arc)

- TIG (Tungsten Inert Gas) Welder uses an electrode that is non-consumable, the shielding gas is externally supplied, and the filler rod is consumable

Stick welders are easy to operate, but they require frequent electrode replacement, which can be frustrating if your job requires you to make plenty of welds. On the other hand, it works well on looser metal or thicker welds. You may have to practice a little since beginners often struggle to get the electrode to "stick" to the workpiece. Welders use a wire feed or MIG process that can produce splatter metal, which must be removed with a grinder to provide a smooth finish around the weld. Whenever possible, it is best for the welded area to be free of paint, dirt, and other obstructions. Welding thicker metal is difficult unless you purchase an expensive machine. Despite being difficult to operate, a TIG welder typically produces excellent results. You'll need to coordinate your hands and feet simultaneously, so if you play the drums, you're already ahead! For a TIG welder to make good welds, the metal needs to be clean. It is best to use a MIG welder for when you are building the container home yourself.

The Hobart model is a great 110-volt MIG welding machine. It is important to note that 110-volt welders frequently have trouble welding metal more than three-sixteenths of an inch thick. You should use a 220-volt welder if you have access to 220 volts of electricity. A dual voltage MIG welder will handle both voltages. The stick welder is an excellent choice if you plan to weld thicker metal (like corner castings on a container) and you don't want to spend a fortune on a high-end MIG machine. It doesn't matter what type of welder a contractor uses if you're planning to hire them for the welding. You should be crystal clear about your expectations regarding surface finish and the amount of welding you will require so that they can choose the best device for your home.

Insulation Kit with Spray Foam

To decide if you need to use spray foam insulation, you need to know what type of insulation you will be using; however, I recommend spray foam insulation. Do note that you still have to decide whether to hire a contractor or build your container home yourself in most cases. You might not want to consider the DIY solution if you are building a small residential house or cabin out of one container.

Pre-mixed solutions are available as sprayable cylinders. A typical kit includes everything you need to install your insulation, including spray nozzles, hoses, and chemicals that create foam. I recommend this kit as one of the best, but keep in mind that you will need several of them to cover your walls, ceilings, and floors (I generally recommend at least two inches of foam).

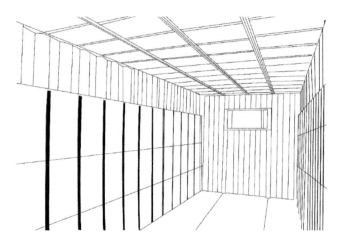

To compare the cost of a DIY option to an estimate from a local contractor, you should reach out to a few local contractors to get an estimate. DIY becomes less economical as the number of containers in the project increases, which means more insulation will be required.

Tools For Cutting Metal

You will use a metal cutter during your build as it is one of the most common tools. To cut windows and doors into your container and to remove any walls you don't need, you will need a metal cutter. There are three main types of tools you can use: an angle grinder, a plasma cutter, or a cutting torch. You shouldn't look past the angle grinder if you're seeking a cheap and DIY-friendly device. You can buy replacement cutting discs for less than a few dollars, and they're easy to operate. With no previous experience required, you can quickly become comfortable using it. Using a grinder with high amperage like a DeWalt unit, you can penetrate container walls with relative ease. You must install the right type of disc since cutting discs are thinner than grinding discs. Better yet, use diamond-impregnated steel discs for long-lasting cutting, which will spare you from frequently replacing the discs. Using a longer-lasting blade can make a world of difference for owners who routinely go through more than 100 traditional cutter disks on one single build with multiple containers. It is best to know that, in addition to being somewhat heavy and generating a lot of gyroscopic force, this tool will wear out your forearms fairly quickly if you use it a lot. Additionally, it's loud and creates lots of sparks, so wearing ear and eye protection is essential.

If you want a clean, smooth cut with little effort, then a plasma cutter is the right choice for you. With a plasma cutter, you'll make cleaner cuts with fewer physical demands than with an angle grinder. Plasma cutters, however, are quite expensive and are probably overkill for a simple container build unless you plan on using one for other projects.

An oxygen or acetylene cutting torch is the last possible option. Although cutting torches are cheaper and faster than plasma cutters, they can be very hard to set up and operate. Getting the settings just right is essential to avoid having a lot of cut slag left after you've finished cutting. Unless you're already well-versed in using cutting torch capabilities, we don't recommend getting one.

Graphics Software

Drawing programs allow us to model and design different ideas for shipping container homes. Drawing and designing a container home does not require computer software, but we find it to be much easier. You can find several tools online that let you draw whatever design you want for your home. Not all of them come packaged as software, some of them can simply be used via a web browser. The program might be too difficult to use on a slow computer, so you might get frustrated. Additionally, you can download design apps for iPads and Android tablets. If you don't want to use a computer, you can simply start sketching on paper and do it that way. As soon as you have completed your drawings, you can scan them and store them on your computer for safekeeping and sharing.

Lifting Equipment

Depending on how you've designed your build, you may need something to lift and place the shipping containers on your foundation when they are delivered to your land. You will be able to choose a foundation type depending on your access to the land and the type of foundation you use. The driver can back directly up to the foundation slab and slide the containers right off if your foundation is built on slabs and there is good access to your site when the containers are being delivered.

The container will likely need to be physically lifted and placed down by a machine, however. Cranes, forklifts, and other equipment can be used to accomplish this. As a crane operator, it's important not to exceed the capacity on the load chart, which is driven by the weight of the lifting apparatus as well as the distance from the crane to the lifting apparatus. Usually, you won't need to worry about this, but there are plenty of videos about crane disasters on YouTube, so triple check all your plans and be extremely careful during the lift.

You will likely need to pay several hundred dollars a day to rent any of these, and even more if there is no nearby option.

Floor Plan

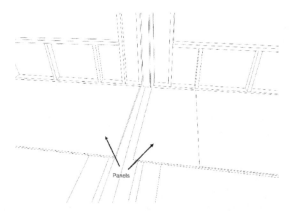

After you've completed all of the most challenging steps, it's finally time to get pumped up about your container home. If you are choosing a floor plan, you should consider the following:

1. Your budget
2. The number of bedrooms
3. The number of bathrooms
4. The Dimensions (how much space you need)
5. Your customizing & upgrading options

Building Your Container Home

You'll receive your final quote and final price once you've selected your floor plan, upgrades, and customizations. You will need to review and sign the sales contract once you approve the final quote. Before the construction of your container, you will have to transfer part of the money.

Get Loan Approval

Please note that the following are just suggestions. To find out how your local bank processes payments, you will need to contact them. Traditional loans (15 years or 30 years) are available through mortgage lenders but are less easy to get through local banks. You can, however, find a mortgage lender by searching online or asking your local bank for recommendations. A pre-approval letter is required after you have chosen a mortgage lender who specializes in lending on modular or manufactured homes. You need this for your construction loan application and your budget.

Construction loans are typically procured through local banks with whom you have a relationship or who are located in the area of construction. Construction loans enable upfront cash for acquiring land, building a house, and making improvements to the site. Loans of this type allow construction progress to be paid from the beginning to the end. A construction loan is usually converted to a permanent mortgage once the home is near completion, and you can contact the mortgage lender that you got your pre-approval letter from for more information. They will give you the best advice on how this works.

Get a Permit

After you have decided on the budget, it is time for you to move on to the next important phase. Now you just need a permit. You should start by contacting your local city or county building department. Does your city or county allow shipping container homes? Prepare yourself for the next few steps if a permit is needed for shipping container homes. The container home will likely have to be certified at this point because it is a manufactured/modular home. Not every state allows for the building of container homes, so you need to see if your area allows its contractors to build these homes or not. Once you get a permit, you are free to move to the next step.

Apply for a Permit Online

Online applications are possible as long as you know which department to send them to. The municipality might be able to help you out as a result. During this session, you will gain a better understanding of what the regulations of your local area are regarding shipping container homes, as well as what it takes to get one built. Having completed your home design and collected all of the required information, you can begin to collect permits and start your permit application online. No matter what kind of permit you need, obtaining one takes a lot of time and patience. Permits can be obtained online through several sources. If you are sending an eligible permit, keep all the required documents with you. Consequently, your local legislation should have already approved all of your projects.

Choose a Location

It's your money that is at stake, so you should decide where your container home should be placed. Locate all the best sites where your container home will be housed. You can then begin looking for a property (unless you own it already) after consulting the city or county. The following factors should be considered when looking for properties:

- Is there a homeowners' association in the area? To find out if a container home is allowed, what is expected in terms of the exterior look, and whether there is a minimum size, you should contact the homeowner's association.

- Are utilities available for this property? Budget-wise, it's essential to know if a property has access to sewers, water, and electricity. Otherwise, a well may need to be drilled for water, sewage will need to be pumped, and electricity will need to be provided by solar cells or a generator. It is probably worth exploring each utility's cost if it is already there or if you must install it.

You should make sure that the highway is easily accessible from your home and also get an idea of what kind of convenience stores are in the local area. You need to make sure that the location has all the necessities that a common house requires and, once your search is finished, you may proceed to the next step.

Contact The Contractor

Lastly, you need to find a contractor who can build the home for you. Your contractor can also help in finding the right location for you and finding all the necessary things near the location. Having selected the property, you now need to contact your chosen general contractor. Get bids from a few general contractors now if you have not done so already and check to see if their schedule is conducive to your timeline. The phase where you select your final design should also occur while you are working with the general contractor. Below is a list of things you might need your contractor's help completing:

- The delivery of your new shipping container home.

- The installation of your driveway. You should make sure the driveway installed with your new home can withstand the delivery load.

- To make final utility connections to the home, the plumber and electrician will need to be called back by the general contractor once the container is set.

- Additionally, all dirt work and grading will be completed by the contractor. You will be able to move into your new home once they receive a final occupancy permit from the city or county.

- They can also get your permit approved. You should never rush when choosing a contractor. Make a bid and see how many contractors are close to that bid, then see how many are willing to strike a deal or negotiate with you.

Container Home Laws in the USA

Among the most affordable home building methods in the USA, shipping container homes may be right for many potential homeowners. You need to make sure that building such a home is legal in the state where you live before including it on your wish list. A shipping container home may be legal or illegal in your state, which brings us to our next topic.

Shipping containers can be used to build homes in most US states. Most of the states that do not allow it just yet have begun to consider it and even intend to find ways to regulate it properly. Keep in mind that even though your state may permit the use of shipping containers, your city or county may not. To ensure compliance with these laws, consult your local authorities. Your county or city planner will be able to provide you with information regarding the legal terms in your area of residence. You still need to follow the local zoning regulations and building codes if you obtain approval from the planner to build a shipping container home.

Shipping Container Zoning

State zoning governs the areas where buildings can be built in every state in the US. Buildings can be erected in different types of zones depending on where they are. The zones are created in such a way that they will contribute to the development of a city harmoniously and follow the municipality's plans. There are exceptions to this rule, such as Houston, which has no zoning. It is therefore a good idea to check your area's zoning code before you begin your shipping container home project. Your future house's design will depend on what kinds of buildings are allowed in the zoning code.

Shipping Container Building Codes

You should also focus on building codes in addition to zoning. In the event of building something in a certain area, it is extremely important to follow a code that specifies what standards should be followed. So, you will not be able to construct a building that does not respect the building codes in the area where the structure is going to be constructed. As part of the building permit application process, you will need to demonstrate that you will adhere to the building code of the municipality where you are planning to build your shipping container home. You must provide proof of compliance before you can receive the necessary approval.

The International Residential Code and International Building Code are, in general, the US building codes. You should also check these codes before you start your building project as they can change once a year or twice every two years. In some states, shipping container homes must meet their building codes, so you will have to check the building codes before setting up your design.

CHAPTER 6:

Why Should You Live in a Shipping Container Home?

A shipping container might not seem like a very appealing house from the outside. Still, when a container home is well-designed, its interior is mind-blowing. Your home will have several benefits if you buy a shipping container. Living in one of these containers is the best decision you can make.

Affordable

Compared to building a house from scratch, shipping container homes are very inexpensive. Because you already have the steel shell of the shipping container home, it's somewhat premade. During the cutting process, you will only need to remove sections for doors and windows. Other features to consider when building a tiny house include flooring, insulation, cabinets, and kitchen appliances.

The traditional way of building a house involves getting the materials, constructing the foundation, fixing the walls, and finally fitting the roof. A special traditional break-in-home will require more resources than one constructed with shipping containers. Shipping container homes are also affordable compared to traditional homes, and there are many on the market. Depending on your interior design choices, the price of a small house can vary greatly, but why pay more when you can have an affordable yet comfortable tiny house?

Portable

Would you consider moving to a beachfront home in the summer? Do you prefer different seasons, or do you feel like moving to different regions? You can live anywhere you want with a shipping container home. A shipping container home is a mobile home with endless placement possibilities. Moving your home from one place to another is possible with a flat-bed truck. It may even be possible for you to tow your house on a trailer. A portable container home is best bolted since welding makes it more permanent. Bolting can be easily detached from the ground or foundation and moved to your desired location. A shipping container home builder can give you more information about how to build your new tiny home.

Customization of Designs

The ability to customize shipping containers is a big advantage for homeowners. Bay windows and stairs can be added, and you can even expand your home. When designing your home, you should take factors such as functionality and climate into consideration. According to your preferences, you can have a multi-story house, a bungalow-style house, or a subterranean house. Shipment container homes come in a limitless variety of designs. However, if you want to make sure you choose the correct design, consult a professional architect.

Off-Site Construction

Permanent structures are not allowed in some locations. A shipping container home's biggest selling point is that you can build them off-site and then load them onto your plot of land. As long as your dream house is already finished, you're not restricted to where construction takes place. When the workers are unavailable in your area, off-site construction is essential. Construction and delivery of your house can be handled by workers. You shouldn't have to worry about the construction process if you already have shipping container home plans. You can also save resources by using off-site construction. Materials and laborers usually need to be transported, but shipping container homes allow for construction to take place near the materials and the workforce.

A Safer Environment

These homes are most commonly found in rural areas. Concern for your safety is normal. It is frequently the case that rural and remote infrastructure is at greater risk of break-ins.

Intruders have a much harder time breaking into steel containers. They are, of course, made of a sturdy material, which makes it hard for someone to quickly break in. There can be no comparison between the number of burglaries in modern homes and container homes because the latter are less attractive to criminals.

CHAPTER 7:

Advantages of
Shipping Container Homes

Both homeowners and landlords are becoming increasingly interested in shipping container homes as an affordable alternative to traditional rental housing. Shipping container properties have many pros, but also some cons.

Sturdy

Using steel containers as a permanent, low-cost home is a great choice because they are durable and easy to build. Using specific floor materials and adding proper insulation in wall and ceiling cavities will improve the efficiency of your home's ventilation and heating systems. Properly oriented windows and sliding glass doors allow for adequate sunlight exposure. A well-built steel container home will likely last a lifetime if it is well designed and constructed.

Ecological

Due to the high cost of returning an empty shipping container after shipment, most shipping companies do not build new containers, resulting in millions of old shipping containers lying unused. Recycling shipping containers to create container homes reduces waste, uses recycled materials, and provides a durable alternative.

Economical

A shipping container home can be built for as little as a few thousand dollars. Because shipping containers are inexpensive, they are a great option for those who would like to build a very basic home. 20-foot containers typically cost $1,500 to $3,000 per unit, while 40-foot containers cost between $3,500 and $4,500. With this structure, building a tiny home can cost you several thousand dollars in containers alone. There are now container homes that are bigger than 2,000 square feet, however, the containers are about $25,000, so if you want a more substantial house, you could be looking at a price higher than that. Compared to traditional wood construction of the same size, this may seem like an enormous leap, but the cost of materials is still minimal.

Modifiable

Customized container homes are extremely flexible. Container construction is becoming a specialty for designers. Using recycled materials, adding sliding glass doors for full walls, and adding off-grid components such as solar panels are some of the ways they offer innovative container architecture designs.

CHAPTER 8:

How to Prepare Your Land for Your Shipping Container Home

Now before your shipping container arrives, you need to decide where you are going to build your home. Preparing the land is the priority that you must sort out. You need to see the ground and the soil that is going to hold your containers together. The type of foundation for a house should be determined by the type of ground and elevation. This will prevent moisture from damaging its contents or causing corrosion. For a single shipping container, a foundation can consist of concrete or a wooden pedestal, or it can consist of a basement for multiple shipping containers.

You must consider both the structural requirements and your preferences when making this decision. Plan to embed steel plates into the concrete where the corner blocks will rest if you choose a poured concrete foundation. The concrete foundations can then be directly welded to the shipping containers.

When planning to use multiple storage containers, it's best to speak with an expert. You might consider options such as a concrete slab, steel plates, concrete piers, and concrete strips. In addition, you should ensure your shipping container is delivered on a clear path. There are many types of foundations, but the four common types for the foundation of container homes are as follows:

- Pier
- Pile
- Slab
- Strip

Pier Foundation

There are many reasons why shipping container homes are built on pier foundations. The foundations are relatively inexpensive, easy to build, and quick to install. A solid concrete block makes up a pier foundation. The concrete blocks, or piers, are generally 50 cm by 50 cm by 50 cm and contain reinforcement steel to improve the strength of the concrete in tension.

A concrete pier is generally positioned at each corner of a shipping container home. Additionally, two extra piers can be placed on each side of the 40-foot container for larger containers. Pier foundations save you a lot of time and money because you don't need to excavate much soil. There is only one thing you have to excavate: the piers, which are usually 50 cm by 50 cm by 50 cm. In comparison, a slab foundation requires excavation beneath the container in its entirety. Furthermore, very few DIY builders have the necessary equipment to build a pile foundation, which is another great reason to use a pier foundation. I recommend this foundation to most people because it is by far the most popular shipping container foundation.

Pile Foundations

When the soil is not strong enough to support the weight of a concrete base, piles are used. There are two types of foundations covered here, but this is the most expensive. The Graceville Container Home was built on pile foundations. The piles (cylinders of solid steel tubes) are driven through the soft ground until they reach more suitable bearing soil. A concrete block is traditionally used to cap the piles after they have been put in place. Once all the piles have been secured, you're left with a grid of concrete caps that above-ground look like concrete pilings. DIY builders should avoid pile foundations. The specialized equipment needed for pile foundations, such as the pile driver, necessitates the use of a contractor.

Slab Foundation

In cases where the ground is soft and an even distribution of weight is required, slab foundations are a popular choice. The downside is that they are more time-consuming and expensive to build than pier foundations. Be prepared to dig a lot if you are using a slab foundation! Slab foundations are concrete slabs upon which you place your containers. A slab foundation generally takes up a little more space than your home's footprint. A slab foundation will be 18 feet by 42 feet if you are building with two 40-foot shipping containers. The foundation would be able to reach up to your shipping containers' perimeter via overhanging feet.

Using slab foundations eliminates the possibility of a hollow foundation due to their solid base. Future termite infestation is prevented in this way. Although slabs are cheaper than pier foundations, concreting them and excavating so much ground makes them more expensive. Plating a foundation in a warmer climate does not pose a freezing risk. When ground temperatures drop below interior temperatures, however, these structures do increase the potential for heat loss. Heat can be conducted in the ground through the container, which transfers more heat than through convection. When the concrete has set, it is impossible to reach utility lines from slab foundations. To gain access to a water pipe that leaks, you will need to cut the concrete. Your utility lines can always be accessed with pier foundations.

Strip Foundation

Strip foundations (also called trench foundations) are similar to pier and slab foundations and consist of a narrow strip of concrete laid to support containers. Concrete strips are usually between two and four feet wide and deep. Instead of going around the perimeter of the containers, the strip could be laid at the tops and bottoms. If you want to build a slab foundation but the ground is not as firm as you would like, this is an ideal solution.

Rubble strip foundations can be constructed where the ground remains damp because of heavy rain. Loose stone can be used below the concrete strip in these situations. As the water runs through the stone, it drains away. All types of foundations have their strengths and weaknesses, including strip foundations. A strip foundation, for example, has a low resistance to earthquakes. Additionally, strip foundations tend to be best suited for smaller and medium-sized buildings due to their shallow form.

Concrete Strength and Your Foundation

This section is extremely relevant if you chose a concrete pier or slab foundation. People who decide to use concrete foundations are often unsure about the concrete strength. The geotechnical engineer's report will determine the strength of concrete you need for your foundation. The C value is the strength of the concrete. One part cement, two parts sand, and five parts gravel are used to make C15 concrete, a general-purpose concrete. Stronger concrete is made with higher cement proportions. Concrete C30, for example, is very strong and contains one part cement, two parts sand, and three parts gravel.

You can mix small quantities either manually or by using a cement mixer if you are mixing small quantities. Purchasing concrete in bulk, ready to use, is a viable option for any size order exceeding one cubic meter. Be sure to thoroughly mix all the elements if you are mixing the concrete yourself, otherwise, the strength of the concrete is greatly reduced. Calculate the cubic meters of your foundation to determine how much concrete you need. Calculate the area by multiplying the depth by the width. You would multiply 10 x 22 x 2 if you wanted to calculate the concrete needed for a slab foundation that is 10-feet wide, 22-feet long, and 2-feet deep. 440 cubic feet of concrete would therefore be required.

The curing process begins as soon as the water is added to the cement. As a result, the concrete will be stronger and more durable if it has been allowed to cure properly. It is very important to keep the concrete's temperature within a range that is suitable for curing (see the concrete's packaging). Generally, the concrete cures in five to seven days. Keep it moist during this period.

Concrete in Hot Weather

Concrete pouring in hot weather requires careful preparation of the area before the concrete is poured. A temporary sunshade should be placed over the concrete to block any direct sunlight. It is also a good idea to spritz the ground with cold water before you lay the concrete. Pour the cold water into the mixing bucket while you mix the concrete. To avoid peak temperatures, one should pour the concrete in the evening or in the morning before dawn.

Concrete in Cold Weather

Concrete pouring during cold weather requires special precautions, just as pouring concrete in hot weather does. Cold weather is characterized by temperatures below zero for at least three consecutive days. Make sure you clean off the forms and base of the concrete before you pour it. Water should be removed from the area. Concrete should be covered with insulation as soon as it is laid. When the concrete is curing, use this time to lay the blankets. To prevent concrete cracking from rapid temperature changes, remove the blankets gradually after the concrete has cured.

Attaching Shipping Containers to the Foundation

In most cases, containers are attached to foundation pads via a steel plate. A welded anchor plate is pressed into the wet concrete with a cast-in-place option. It is also possible to epoxy anchors into concrete after it has hardened. It is also possible to use mechanical anchors, but these are typically weaker and are not recommended. The concrete plate needs to be flat and level so that the four corners of the containers can be fitted to it. Concrete is placed on steel plates and shipping containers are placed on top. Welding is done after everything has sealed. The containers may simply be placed on the foundations (their heavy weight holds them in place). It is probably fine in most cases, but floods and tornadoes can move loose containers.

CHAPTER 9:

Insulation of Container Homes

There are different kinds of insulation used for container homes. A few of them are emerging insulations that are gaining popularity. These insulations include the following:

Spray Foam Insulation

With spray foam insulation, you can insulate a container home easily and quickly. In addition to the exterior walls of a shipping container, this insulation material can also be sprayed onto the interior walls. Many shipping containers are painted with highly toxic paint, but the VOCs that are released into the atmosphere can be trapped by spray foam insulation. Polyurethane spray foam insulation has also been linked to respiratory ailments like asthma, pneumonia, and lung damage, as well as possible health hazards. Additionally, you should be aware that not all spray foam is created equal. Many conventional spray foams can negatively impact the environment. Spray foam insulation called Icynene has plastic bubbles inside it that insulate the home as it hardens. This foam product is blown over water causing it to expand and harden. Unlike other types of polyurethane spray foam, Icynene insulation is unlikely to disperse any VOCs into the air for at least two weeks after installation.

Fiberglass

Fiberglass is the most commonly used insulation material found in walls, floors, and ceilings that are unfinished. Although readily available and relatively inexpensive, it is prone to rot, mold, and poor indoor air quality, which may eventually cause damage to metal structures.

Cotton Insulation

Trying to reuse as much material as possible is an important aspect of sustainable homes and construction. Some companies now offer recycled, cotton-based insulation made from used jeans and cotton that has been recycled post-consumer. R-values for cotton insulation are similar to those for fiberglass insulation. Boric acid, a natural fire retardant, is usually used on commercial denim insulation. In addition to the heat gain of denim, a vapor barrier is needed. The material becomes dense, loses some of its insulation properties, and takes a long time to dry after getting wet. Among the companies offering denim insulation that is VOC-free and made from recycled post-consumer waste is Ultra Touch.

Wool Insulation

In addition to sheep's wool, there are other natural insulation alternatives such as cellulose. Fiberglass, denim, or other fibrous insulation types also have an R-value of 3.5 per inch, which is comparable to this environmentally friendly and high-performance alternative. In addition to natural flame retardants, sheep wool contains lanolin, which does not require further chemical treatment.

Cork Insulation

Several natural insulation alternatives exist for container homes, including cork insulation. Biodegradable and renewable, cork is a product of trees. The bark from cork trees is harvested every nine years instead of cutting down trees to harvest the cork. Due to the cork forest (mostly in Portugal) capturing carbon from the atmosphere during this harvesting process, cork is considered "carbon negative."

A cork shipping container home also benefits from its acoustic property. By installing this natural insulation material between your home and the metal walls of the container, it will prevent sound from being transmitted easily between the two. Companies like ThermaCork make these products.

CHAPTER 10:

How to Plan Your Shipping Container Home

Before starting a project, you must have a proper plan. This will help you to execute it successfully and get positive results. This applies to building a shipping container home; you must have a plan in your mind or sketch it out in a planner or notebook. With this, you can get assistance in building a home within your budget. Five crucial things come into view while planning for building a shipping container home. Stick to these and you are good to go:

- Set a budget
- Select, customize, and finalize the design
- Choose where you want to build your home
- Decide who will build your home
- Finalize: Is it feasible?

Setting a Budget

Setting a spending plan is crucial; it will help you to anticipate the total cost you have to spend on the construction of the house. Also, it will help you to set a range limit so as not to spend an extra penny. Moreover, you will be able to construct your house on a limited budget. The constructors you are dealing with may also request a plan if you have one. If you don't, they could make their own, but that could be expensive for you. So, be prepared beforehand in all terms. For example, if you have a budget of $50,000 and you want to construct a 4000 square feet house, it doesn't make sense at all, and it isn't the way to do it.

First, you must create a rough architecture plan, which includes the decided dimensions of the plot of your container home. Then, consider the following things in your budget plan to create a rough estimation. This will help you to not exceed the limit in between or at the end of the construction process.

- Property costs
- Foundation costs
- Project management costs
- Costs of materials used in construction
- Professional fees
- Labor costs
- Tools and equipment costs

Select, Customize, and Finalize the Design

Design is as important as the stability and foundation of the house. Designing container homes is quite easy and can be a fun, creative task. While planning a budget, it might be possible that you have already drawn a design or structure draft in your mind during the brainstorming process. Now it's time to put it into action. The design depends upon the layout, and you have to decide on the layout of your house according to your own needs. Whether you want to build a single-container home or a large mansion with many containers is up to you!

If you put the right questions and queries into focus while planning the design, it might help you to avoid the expenses. If you want to change the design both outside and inside halfway through, then all your money will be wasted, so be vigilant.

Select the Place Where You Want to Build Your Home

After brainstorming on deciding the budget and making a structure for the house, the next crucial step is to decide the place where you want to construct your shipping container home. Many places are costly, so you'll have to find the right balance between spending money on the location and spending money on the construction of your home. For this, there is no need to worry so much since you can check websites online to find a suitable and affordable location. Search on Zillow, for example – maybe you can find something there, or you can go ahead and search outside by yourself. Finding a local area is also a good option if you are on a mission to stay strictly within your budget. These are the places that often promote sales. You must remember that after researching and buying the property, you also have to get registered and be granted permission to build a container home there.

Decide Who Will Build Your Home

To save on costs, you may have taken on the task of making the structure of the house by yourself and have already decided on the budget. But now you have to lay down your arms. What I mean is that you have to hire someone to construct your container home – someone who is very professional. You can't take the risk of building it and having it last for only a few years. Of course, you want a home with a lifetime guarantee, or at least as many years as it can stay durable. On the other hand, if you want to build your home by yourself to save money, you must make sure you have the practical skills or that you have learned some before starting the construction. It all depends on you!

While looking for a contractor, you have to think of the following things and then finalize a contract with them.

- Do they provide a guarantee?

- Do they give any references?

- What are their experiences and their skills?

- Do they have liability insurance?

- How much will they charge?

- How long will it take for them to complete the construction of the house?

Finalize: Is Your Shipping Container Home Feasible?

After planning and deciding on the location, the contractor, use of materials, and the total amount of money, now is the time to make a final decision. Decide how much time it will take; does it stand within the means of the budget that you set before sketching a plan? If so, then you're on your way to constructing your container home!

CHAPTER 11:

Mistakes to Avoid When Building a Shipping Container Home

You may be overwhelmed after learning about the merits of container homes, like affordability, flexibility, and sturdiness, and now you are on the way to building your own home. However, you may need to pause for a moment. This is because when planning, there are very obvious mistakes you can make, and these can lead to disaster if they are not addressed. So, it is better to know what those mistakes are and avoid them while building a shipping container home.

Buying Containers in Bad Condition

If you are building a container home, considering the condition of the containers is of utmost importance. If you buy a container or all containers in bad condition, then it will negatively impact you in the end. You then have to spend money to repair them, or they may even reach a point where they are beyond repair. For example, if you buy a container in the wrong condition (for example, if it is corroded or rusted), then you have to do a lot of work to weld and cut metal out of the rusted part. Moreover, you will also have to polish it for a better touch-up.

Another thing to consider is whether the container offers enough sturdiness for building a home as they are the foundation of building a sustainable and strong home. If you are thinking of buying second-hand containers, then check the grading condition of the containers. Or, if you are buying from an online shop, it is still advisable to first have a look at the condition of the containers as the images won't show the exact quality, they are in.

Using the Wrong Size Shipping Container

Besides choosing a good, conditioned container, it's important to choose the right size of container because the wrong choice can waste your money and also create problems when you are measuring the dimensions and building a home. Another thing to consider is that all containers should be the same height to build a roof for the whole container home at the same level. If you have no idea about the dimensions, you can consult a planner or conduct thorough research before buying.

Building on Poor Foundations

We have already discussed how to lay the foundation of a shipping container home, so, if someone still thinks that container homes do not require a foundation, or this is not a worthy or crucial topic to discuss for building a container, then they're wrong. Whether you are making a traditional home with bricks and cement or a container home, a solid foundation is always necessary. If you don't consider the foundation, then your steel house won't be able to withstand hurricanes and other natural disasters.

A concrete foundation will give stability to your house and will also increase durability. You cannot simply place the containers on the ground; instead, you should build a concrete foundation if you want to make your container home into a permanent residence. You must consider which materials will help in building a strong base for your house or how deep you have to dig in the mud. Keep other factors in view, like your time and money. Most importantly, focus so that these materials do not contribute to increasing the condensation in the base.

Cutting Extra Steel Out of Containers

If you buy old or used containers for your home building, then they may be worn out or have corroded edges. So, to remove the corroded part, you may cut the steel to give it a new look and protect the remaining part from damage. Here you have to take care if you are cutting the right amount of required steel or more. It not only costs you money for cutting and welding purposes but also affects or decreases the size of the container. If this happens, you will have to buy a new container. Also, it can affect the integrity and structure of your home. In addition, if you buy a new container but want a lot of customization, you can ask a builder to cut it to give your home a different layout. The steel container will then undergo modifications that take a lot of time and effort.

Not Considering Planning Regulations

How will you feel when you have to lay down the foundation of your home because you have not followed the planning regulations and your time, effort, and money have all been wasted? Yes. Wherever you plan to build or whichever type of home, traditional or a container home, some rules and regulations will exist in that location. Without considering those rules, you cannot establish your new home. Firstly, there is a need to have thorough research about those rules, and then you must follow them. If you face any inconvenience in following the rules, you may have to discuss with the local council of that area. This will help you to resolve the matter or remove the hurdles you are facing in building a home. You have to complete the procedure of buying the land and making deals with the local committee so that in the future, after building a house, you won't face any issues and can live a happy life.

Not Understanding Building Codes

The building codes are the rules to ensure that nothing is done while building a house that can harm the environment and the nearby surroundings. Even if you are the only one building a home at that place, you still have to understand all the building codes and get permits. You must follow all relevant structural, local, and environmental codes or else you can't establish your home.

Signing contracts is not cost-free; you have to pay money for such agreements as these are the laws.

For example, if you establish a home in any area of the USA, certain laws will give you a permit to build a home. If you do not do this, you will get charged for neglecting the laws, and they'll also stop your construction. If the home is completed, they can also demolish it. So, avoid this mistake and make necessary documents, sign them, email them, and keep the record with you. Take note that this consent process is very crucial.

Neglecting to Budget for Contingencies

Plan your budget by keeping possible contingencies in view. You have made a complete map and have decided all the budget and costs of the materials and other things, and you are sure that you can build a home within this budget. But that's not always the case. You have to be ready and have a separate budget for future costs. It may be possible that you want to add something or customize the design, and the new designs may cost more money, or you may set aside a specific amount of money for the insulation but when you go ahead and buy it, you find out that the cost has increased. Oops! But if you have already saved money for such contingencies, then great job! If plan A doesn't work, you have plan B to opt for when you can't find a solution for the problem. Of course, you don't want to stop the construction of your dream house and you don't want to upset your partner.

So, it is best to be prepared for future scenarios in such cases. The market rates for materials keep on changing, and with that, rising figures in dollars for each product, material, or even container can make you angry if you suddenly have to face them unexpectedly. Also, your contractor can charge more, or you might have to spend extra money on the building codes and regulations to follow the laws strictly. That's why it is better to prepare yourself beforehand.

Using the Wrong Type of Insulation

Insulation serves a lot of benefits, so there should be no compromise on this as well. People often choose the wrong insulation that they have to change often, which only contributes to the wastage of money. Even if you choose good insulation, consider the environment of your place because insulation depends on many factors like the climate conditions, budget, age of container, and size of your home.

For instance, a rainy climate will contribute to water damage. Thus, you have to insulate your whole home well without any leakage or else it will drain down the house and into the foundations. You can use spray foam insulation to deal with this. Regions with a dry climate the whole year should use insulation that will keep the interior of the house cool. Insulation will also be a great barrier to condensation and the effects of corrosion in any season. If you can't afford expensive insulation material, you can use eco-friendly newspaper insulation, but that will not be a permanent solution to stop condensation.

Choosing the Wrong Contractor

Choosing the wrong builder or contractor might be the worst mistake you could make. Try to contact someone professional or at least someone who knows about building shipping container homes. If they don't have any DIY knowledge and experience, they cannot build a house perfectly, not even if it is a single container one-room home. Choosing the wrong contractor will cost you a lot of time and money and the construction of the home will not go according to your expectations.

Some contractors don't sign an agreement to build the home till the end. That would be a major mistake because the person who has laid the foundation should build until the end because they know all the estimations, measurements, and materials and the division of costs in all things. Another benefit of choosing an experienced contractor is that they can build your home according to your financial condition.

CHAPTER 12:

Design and Customize Your Shipping Container Home

When you get a chance to build a shipping container home, it's time to conduct thorough research to get ideas, then brainstorm to turn your ideas into reality. Shipping container homes are the easiest ones to build, and they don't require a long period for their construction, nor do you have to spend a huge sum of dollars on building them. However, when it comes to designing and customizing a shipping container home, it requires some effort, money, time, and research. To make it your dream house, you have to spend time thinking about and planning how to make its design unique and customize it to give it an appealing look. So far you have learned how to make it, which materials are used, its benefits, and other necessary information. It's time to move ahead to your final destination – deciding how you can give your home a unique look.

Floor Plans for a Shipping Container Home

Just like traditional houses, you can also choose by selecting and building different floor plans. Even if it is a two-container home, there is no need to worry, you can still make it a paradise for yourself to live in. Here we'll tell you how to turn your fantasies turn into reality. We will now look at several different flooring plans that you can use.

20' 1 Bedroom Container Homes

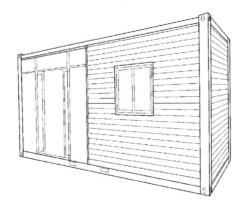

Examples of Possible 20' Container Homes

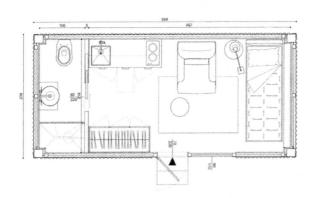

The Professional: 160 Square Feet Floor Plan

If you can't afford to build a big home from many containers, you can build a 160 square feet home. Here you have an all-in-one living room, bedroom, kitchen, and bathroom. There will be no walls. This is the most simple, aesthetic, and minimalistic option. You can give a stylish look by making a sleeping corner at the side, a couch placed in the center, side kitchen shelves, and a side bathroom.

The Weekender: 160 Square Feet Floor Plan

Just like the above professional plan, the Weekender also offers a 160 square foot space to live in. You just have to make one change, which is to give your bathroom a larger surface area.

The Backyard Bedroom: 160 Square Feet Floor Plan

As the name indicates, you have to shift your bedroom to the backyard. You can construct this home with a 20' container. With minimal and efficient finishing, you can give your container house an amazing look. You can build a bathroom on one side, on the other side you can fix a bedroom, and in between, you can make a place to study or relax.

The Bachelorette: 160 Square Feet Floor Plan

This is also a single-person home with a bathroom at one end, a bedroom at the other end, a kitchen in the corner, and a lounge in the center of the house. If you are alone or are a student and plan on living in a container home, then you can choose this one as it has a compact layout.

The Roommate House: 160 Square Feet Floor Plan

If you are planning to live with your friends, then this floor plan can be the best choice. This is built with just one 20' container and helps you save your money. There is a single main door. The bathroom doesn't have a door, instead, it has stairs. Also, there are stairs above the open kitchen. The central lounge space also serves as a bedroom.

The Six Person Bunk House: 160 Square Feet Floor Plan

This plan has four bunks arranged one above the other. As this is a small area home, built with just one 20' container, you cannot get a lounge. However, you can change the area to 320 square feet to include space for a lounge, kitchen, and bathroom.

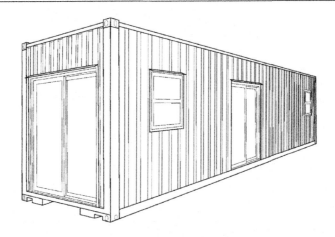

The Empty Nester: 1 Bedroom 320 Square Feet Floor Plan

You can construct this with a 40' container. It means it would be a long, rectangular home with a large space. You can place a lot of accessories and appliances inside this home. Also, you can build a large kitchen and a wide bedroom. In addition, you can install a bathtub in the bathroom.

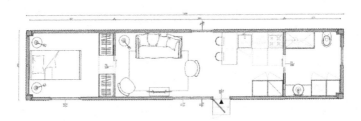

The Pioneer: 2 Bedroom 320 Square Feet Floor Plan

You can construct a pioneer home with a 40' container. This too will be a rectangular-shaped home, but it will have more length and space. You can also make a double bedroom here and a separate living room with a wall between the bedroom and lounge. A spacious open kitchen can be attached to the lounge.

Also, a large bathtub can be placed in the bathroom.

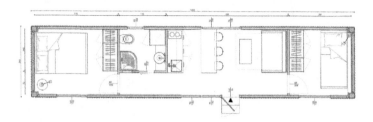

The Double Bunk Home: 320 Square Feet Floor Plan

This house is for friends or roommates, and it is structured to look like a room with many bunk beds. It serves as a place for four bunk beds: two with one above the other on one corner, and two on the other corner. Both have two central bathrooms and two kitchens alongside the rooms. There are also two main gates.

The Four Person Bunk House: 320 Square Feet Floor Plan

This is also for four people; the beds are arranged in a bunk one above the other. All four beds are separated by a closet. The kitchen and bathroom are located at the other corner. The central space is open and can be adjusted as a lounge or for study purposes.

Two 20' Container Homes

The Happy Together House: Two Bedroom 320 Square Feet Floor Plan

This home is for two people or a couple to live in and can be constructed easily, but you will have to use two containers of 20' to make it a wide and square home with plenty of space so that you can easily place a double bed inside and create walls in between the bedroom and the living room. There can also be a separate spacious kitchen and a large bathroom.

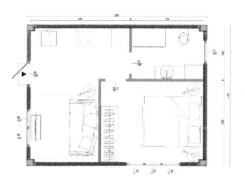

One 20' Container & One 40' Container Home

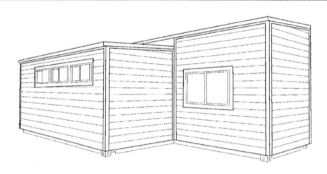

The Dwell: One Bedroom 480 Square Feet Floor Plan

This house is constructed with two containers of size 40' and 20'. The two dimensions are different, so it will neither be a square nor a rectangular-shaped home. It has three separations: one for a spacious bedroom, one for a wide and open lounge, and one for a kitchen with shelves. Near the kitchen, there can be a washroom and a bathroom.

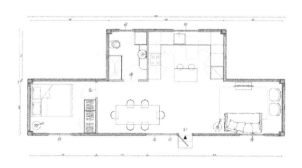

Two 40' Container Homes

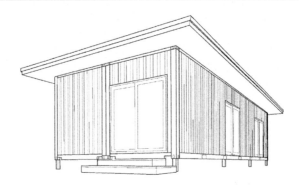

The Duo House: One Bedroom 640 Square Feet Floor Plan

Though the word duo is in the name of this floor plan, it is a single bedroom home. However, it has more space than the previous ones. It is a spacious home set with all the necessary rooms: a large bedroom with an attached bathroom, a walk-in closet, and a large dining space with a sitting lounge. An open kitchen can be attached to the dining area. This home has many gates for different rooms.

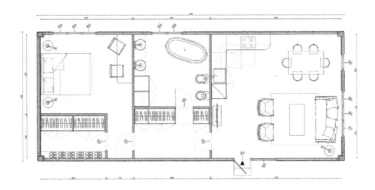

The Double Duo: Two Bedroom 640 Square Feet Floor Plan

This is a similar design to the one above, but with one difference – it has two bedrooms. Both of these bedrooms have two different closets and different gates. There is only one spacious bathroom. Otherwise, it has the same architecture and design as the floor plan above.

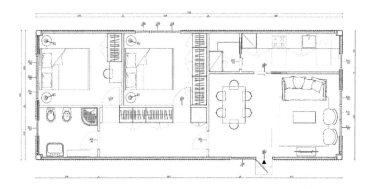

The Four Bedroom Home

This layout can either be in an "L" shape or with the rooms aligned next to each other.

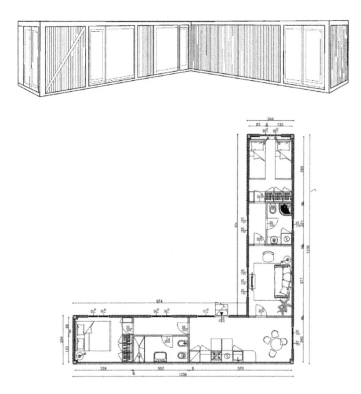

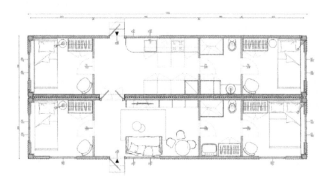

Two 20' Containers & Two 40' Containers Home

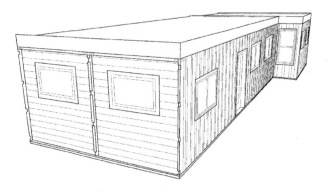

The Family Matters House: Two Bedroom 960 Square Feet Floor Plan

This home is specifically designed for a family with the help of four containers. Having a 960 square feet area, this is a spacious home. Every partition has a large surface area to walk in. It has a central large dining room with a kitchen plus a sitting space with a washroom attached. One bedroom is located at one corner, and the other corner has one more bedroom with a bathroom and a closet.

The Happy Family Home: Three Bedroom 960 Square Feet Floor Plan

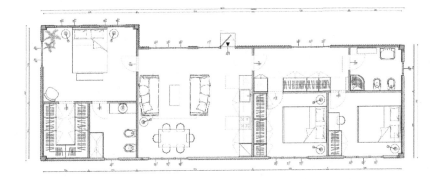

This also has the same area size as the previous floor plan but is adjusted with three bedrooms. Two bedrooms are combined with a central wall and separate doors at one corner of the home.

There is also a bathroom and a lounge. Aside from the lounge, a dining place is set with a spacious and open kitchen. The other bedroom is large with more space and a separate bathroom and closet.

The Luxury Home: Three Bedroom 960 Square Feet Floor Plan

This floor plan also has three bedrooms – two together and one separate. But the layout for this one is different as the shape of the house is also different from the previous two. This is made with four containers. The separate bedroom closet has an opening that leads to the bathroom. The other two have direct closets and a single bathroom outside. The central space is a lounge with an open kitchen.

Other Floor Plan ideas

In case you are not convinced with the floor plans just presented, there are millions of potential combinations. The limit is your creativity. Below are 5 additional beginner-friendly floor plans.

The One Bedroom tower

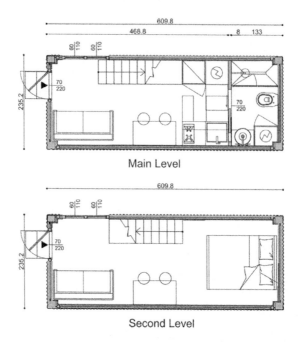

Main Level

Second Level

The Ranch Style Two Bedroom Home

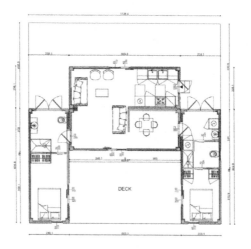

The Budget Ranch Style Two Bedroom Home

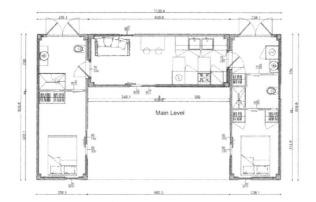

The Aussie Ranch Style Home

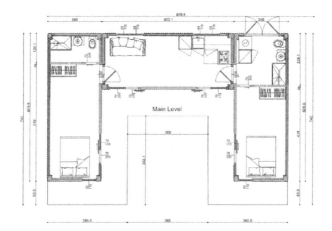

The Canadian Wilderness Style Home

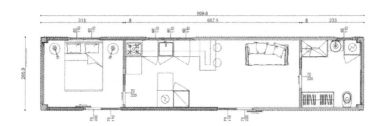

Door Styles for Container Home

Doors are essential for the completion of a house. Also, to stay safe inside the house during the constantly fluctuating temperatures throughout the year, good quality doors are necessary. You can buy a simple door, but when you attach aesthetically designed doors, it increases the beauty of the house. There are countless designs and styles for doors that you can choose for your container home.

3' Residential

This is a windowpane door with a width of 3' of 3' and glass at the center.

Patio Doors

These are relatively expensive doors. If you can afford them, you should buy these unique doors. Generally, the cost for these doors is in the range of $1200 to $10000. These are glass sliding doors with one side fixed while the other one glides.

French Doors

French doors are just like patio doors except they are fully made of glass. These are, however, different from patio doors in a way that they open outwardly on a hinge while the patio doors open by sliding horizontally.

Farmhouse Style

These doors offer a mixture of the old and the modern, with modern aesthetics and an old cultural touch. Though considered vintage, there are chic style farmhouse doors available too. With beautifully layered textures and a clean blend of lines, they give a timeless look to the outside and can also be used inside your home.

Sliding Doors

Sliding doors come in a variety of designs and layouts, all having the common feature of sliding. Such doors are very common and in demand these days. They're also thermally efficient as they have a belt around the edges that keep the inside of the home protected.

Modern Style Doors

Modern style doors include all the variety that comes in this modern era. These are mostly made of different types of wood structures with different finishes and textures. All of these elements add to the aesthetic of the house.

Window Styles for Container Homes

Windows are an important part of the house; you can't build a container home without ventilation. Air space is necessary, and windows serve this purpose. Installing windows in-between the containers is a difficult process, requiring a lot of cutting and welding. Read on to find container home window ideas and styles you can make for your container home. We have described a few window styles; you can select any of these depending upon your budget and requirements.

White Vinyl Windows

These are durable windows with white frames outside the edges. These panes add to the sturdiness of the window. You also don't have to paint them. Another advantage of white vinyl windows is that there is no peeling or cracking of paint. They are thermal protector windows; thus they also serve as energy-efficient panels. The white vinyl paint usually lasts longer – a duration of about 20 to 40 years.

Double-hung Windows

Double-hung windows have two panels hung in the downward direction, one above the other. These open in the outward direction and can also move up and down. Double-hung windows are attached with springs that can control the opening of the window sashes.

Casement Windows

Casement windows have more than one hinge at the point of attachment with a frame that is fixed on a wall. These are the simplest windows and are most widely used both in the old and modern eras. They can be opened both inside and outside – it depends on how you fix them. The sashes are known as casement sashes. They are cheap windows available in the range of $325 to $450.

Fixed Windows

Fixed windows do not have any openings. They are closed and do not allow the entry of air or any other things inside. Though they are good for protection, it is necessary to have some air space that can serve the purpose of ventilation. People mostly use them to let sunlight into the house so that their rooms do not remain dark inside. These are the cheapest windows, and they usually have a price range of $200 to $650.

Roof Styles for Container Homes

Besides customizing the walls, doors, and windows of the container home, it's necessary to have a look at the roof styling. Because the roofs of containers are rough with curves, designing them with some material will help furnish them well. Here we have listed three different styles that can give a classic look to your home, whether it's a one-container roof or a large four-container roof.

Gable Style

Gable roofs are just like huts, with two edges meeting at the upper side while the edges are downwardly structured. They give your container the shape of a hut. To make a gable roof, you first have to cut the container walls in the same dimensions as required according to the roof. It will then be easier and will save you time and money. The pitch of the roof depends on the height of the container or the home.

Sloped Core Style

A sloped core roof is also like a gable roof, but it does not resemble it that much as the slope of this roof depends on the pitch and the angle. These are simpler than gable roofs. A sloped core roof can be the best selection for lofted floor plans. A loft floor house is a house in which there is a lot of space since there are no internal walls. If you are building two container homes without walls, then the sloped core style of roofing can serve a great purpose for both decorative style and coverage.

A Combination of Slope and Gable

A combination of slope and gable? Yes, you heard that right! It is possible to blend both roof types and get a unique architectural style for the roofing. If you are building a two-container home, but both are of different sizes and dimensions, you can opt for the gable roofing for the smaller one and the sloped roofing for the large one. In this way, one house will have a combination of both roof styles.

Exterior Siding Designs

Exterior siding has a lot of benefits. One is the addition of fine touches, increasing the sophistication and aesthetic touch. Another reason for using exterior siding either with windows or doors is that it gives protection to all the panels. The corners of steel containers are usually sharp, so it's necessary to wrap them so that there remain no edges on the outer side. Also, this coverage will help to protect the container from rain and other water damage, ultimately protecting it from corrosion. Here are a few suggestions for exterior siding that are good to use.

LP Smart Lap Siding

LP smart lap siding looks like wood because it is made of wood. Thus, it helps to give the natural cedar look and increases the beauty of the home. Also, it provides excellent resistance and structural support by maintaining the frame of the home. A lot of designs are available for LP smart siding. Some are made of resins and wax, thus there will be less dust when it is time to weld. It's also affordable as the cost of LP smart lap siding is $2 to $4 per square foot. The installation process is also easy.

Cedar Lap Siding

Cedar lap siding is very expensive, ranging between $9000 and $19000 for an entire house, but $6 per square foot. It also depends on how many containers are used in the construction of the home. It's a durable siding as it is made from natural wood that serves a great purpose in strength. Because of this, it is gaining popularity, though it is a bit expensive. Its size is often 6", 8" or maybe between 10" and 12". One disadvantage is it can get dirty and dusty easily, so you have to clean it often with water.

Two-Tone Ribbed Metal

Two-tone ribbed metal siding comes in two colors and materials. You can use two metals for the siding of the home, or you can use one metal for the side of the base floor and use another metal for the upper floor that is above the base floor. This could also be a combination of corrugated iron and wood.

Ribbed Metal Core

Using metal for the metal covering? Yes! It's just like a container. This is named so because of the rib-like structure the container walls have. The structure and finish give a very pleasing look to the container as a whole from the outside. Using ribbed metal also gives other benefits – they are versatile, easily installed, durable, and offer high performance.

Cabinet Designs and Layouts

Imagine your room looks like a storeroom with clothes piled up and other accessories lying here and there. Here the importance of cabinets comes into view. You cannot keep things without placing them in cabinets, whether these are kitchen utensils or your clothes. Shipping container homes are usually small and built in a compact form, so it's necessary to design the layout of the cabinets in a way that can keep everything you need. Make sure to build a closet for your room, a showcase for your lounge, and cabinets in your kitchen too.

Ok, so you have structured the cabinets and now it is time to furnish them. Here are two types of cabinet designs that offer a very pleasing look:

Stained Cabinets

Stained cabinets offer unique style and beauty to your kitchen and also to your lounge area. Stained cabinets give you a more natural look than painted cabinets. If you want to give a natural look to your kitchen, go for stained cabinets.

Painted Cabinets

Painted cabinets make your room look bigger. They give high-end touches to your space. It takes a lot of time to paint the cabinet. Because a perfectly painted cabinet needs at least two coats of paint, you can just buy painted cabinets. Choose the color according to the color theme of your home.

Kitchen Accessories

Building a kitchen in a shipping container home seems like a dream. Though people mostly use such houses for vacation purposes, you still have to have an area for cooking your meals. If you are thinking of just having a table and an electric stove to cook meals on, I would advise you that that would be the wrong choice as you also have to install other accessories that can help you make the cooking process easier. You have to drain the water after washing dishes and you need apparatus like a fire extinguisher in case of emergency. You also have to find a way to remove the smoke. So, head on down to have a look at the essentials of a kitchen.

Under-Cabinet Lighting

Under-cabinet lighting is an important component of a kitchen renovation. It saves us from kitchen accidents which take place due to poor lighting. Cabinet lighting installation is the easiest too. As these lights work on low voltage, lights for cabinets are more efficient than LED lights.

Pots and Pans Drawers

Pots and pans drawers are used to organize your kitchen cookware. They make your kitchen look organized and tidy. These drawers will help you find any cookware more easily. They will also help you with cabinet storage problems. Pans drawers must be 24 inches deep.

Trash Can Drawer

Trash can drawers are used for discarding waste. Trash cans should be placed inside any cabinet to hide them from others because having a visible trash can is not good. There should also be a separate cabinet at the side for trash cans. A large drawer is best for trash cans.

Kitchen Tile Backsplash

A kitchen tile backsplash is an extension to a counter in your kitchen. It helps to protect the sink wall from water. It also helps to protect from food splatter when cooking at high flame and keeps your kitchen clean. Most backsplashes are made up of ceramic or porcelain tile. These tiles are waterproof, so they are easy to clean. A backsplash is a great idea for your kitchen and is also cost-effective.

Bathroom Vanity

Bathroom vanities are important whether it's a traditional brick house or a container home, but their significance increases in a container home. This is because using good vanities will help to keep the bathrooms clean, ensuring a smooth drainage system, and also keep it free from moisture that is necessary to avoid condensation in a container home. Nowadays, these come in a wide range of styles and built-in structures and designs. Hence, besides giving the main benefits, they also serve as iconic furnishing pieces. Here we have listed a few different vanities and their benefits, and you can buy any according to the space of your bathroom and budget.

Granite Sink Bowl

Granite sink bowls are reliable and resistant to damage. These sink bowls are better than steel sinks because they are easy to clean without the use of chemicals. Granite sinks are scratch-resistant. These are best for use in bathrooms due to their long-lasting features. These sinks will also enhance the beauty of your place.

Floating Vanity

The main advantage of a floating vanity is that your rooms will appear larger. They give the illusion that your home has additional space, and they are easy to clean. The floating vanity is a new trend for houses nowadays. There are different designs of floating vanity to use in your bathroom.

Onyx Vanity White Bowl

Nowadays, onyx is used as a bathroom vanity. Due to this vanity, your small bathroom will look elegant and clean and will also look bigger than normal. The stone material is used for onyx white bowls. These bowls have a translucent appearance. You can choose different colors and varieties for these vanity bowls.

Quartz with Under-Mount Sink Bowl

For under-mount sink bowls, quartz is definitely the best to use. Quartz makes these sinks more long-lasting, and it is easy to clean them because there is no border around them. This design is available in six different colors. Quartz sinks add beauty to your bathroom and are perfect for container homes.

CHAPTER 13:

The Flooring of
Your Shipping Container Home

The flooring of shipping container homes is usually made of wood such as Apitong (also known as Keruing) which usually does not have resistance to pest attacks. In fact, they can attract them quite easily. So, it's possible that, with such hardwood floorings, you may allow pests and chemicals inside your home. Changing the flooring can oftentimes increase your budget, so it's better to take care of it sooner than later. Let's look at some other options for flooring that can provide a better solution to these common problems.

Bamboo Flooring

Bamboo flooring is just like plywood flooring, meaning it looks like wood. It is made from a natural bamboo stalk. Having many benefits, people often use it for their container homes. Manufacturers construct or shape the flooring tiles depending on the layout of the house. Bamboo flooring is treated with pesticides so that your home remains pest-free. Pesticides are only used to kill pests – they're not harmful to humans. Also, during the shipping process, they will not be affected by moisture.

This will help retain their original quality for quite some time when they are in a humid place. Using this type of flooring has both advantages and disadvantages.

Pros

1. It is made of renewable material. Hence, it is eco-friendly.
2. This flooring can be maintained easily.
3. Refinishing can also be done easily.

Cons

1. It scratches easily.
2. It also cracks easily if exposed to excess humidity.

Coin Vinyl Flooring

Vinyl flooring is the most commonly used and also the most demanding flooring because of the aesthetic beauty it gives to the home. People like it not only for container homes but also for workplaces. The composition of this type of flooring is mainly polyvinyl chloride resin – that's why you can get a lot of benefits from this flooring (such as no stains and no moisture). When it doesn't catch moisture, then it definitely serves as a durable foundation for flooring. Also, it provides a protective cover against oil acids, dirt, etc. Other than that, it's economical, which is a bonus benefit. It has two shadings: gray or tan. If you have already used plywood covering, you can still roll it out on top of the plywood.

Pros

1. It is water-resistant.
2. It can be installed easily.
3. Maintenance is easy.
4. It is durable.
5. It is affordable.
6. It is unique and beautiful.
7. It is easy to clean and wash with.

Cons

1. It is not resistant to dents.
2. It is non-biodegradable.
3. It decolors or fades quickly.

Epoxy Coating Flooring

Epoxy coating, as the name indicates, is used as a cover. If your old flooring gets rough or dented, then you can use a new covering of epoxy resin flooring. These floorings are good coverings for all types of floorings. They don't just provide sturdiness and durability; they are also resistant to stains. Epoxy coating gives a unique shininess to the surface, increasing the brightness of the place. Also, it doesn't require any maintenance, you just need to make sure to clean it regularly to retain its shine. The glossy surface adds to the aesthetic finishes of the floor as well as the rest of the room. There is no need to put a carpet on this floor as it already adds to the beauty of the living space. However, you cannot use it without a primer and a finishing coat. Apply primer first and leave it for a few hours so that the epoxy coating attaches firmly. Make sure there's no water layer in between.

Pros

1. It is smooth and durable.
2. It is a slip and shock-resistant flooring.
3. It is a less abrasive flooring.
4. It is available in a variety of colors.
5. It is safe and long-lasting.

Cons

1. It is slippery.

2. It may have a strong, fume-like smell.

3. It is sensitive if it is not fixed properly

Aluminum and Steel Flooring

Steel flooring? Sounds strange, right? Well, it's a new era! If you're living in a steel hone, why can't you walk on a steel floor as well? Well, now you can. Besides using aluminum for windows, doors, and other purposes, it is now also used in floorings. Though it is noisy to walk on a steel floor, it serves as a strong foundation. As for aluminum flooring, you can choose between steel with high traction or a smooth finish. Though they are maintained and kept clean easily, the installation of steel and aluminum floorings is very difficult. You cannot use this flooring without a carpet or any insulation because, firstly, it won't look good. Secondly, insulation will help you to maintain the temperature sensitivity of the floor as in the summer, it can heat up easily and in winters, it gets cold easily.

Pros

1. It's durable and adds to the longevity of the floor.

2. It is a low-maintenance flooring.

3. It can be cleaned easily.

4. It has a shining surface.

5. It has high strength.

6. It is safe.

7. It is environmentally friendly.

Cons

1. It is very expensive.

2. Installation is very difficult.

3. There are fewer styles and color options available.

4. It is sound and temperature-sensitive.

Imitation Wood Vinyl Planks Flooring

If you want water-resistant flooring or complete waterproof flooring, then you have an option to choose imitation wood vinyl planks flooring. It will add beauty to your space by giving it a stylish and sophisticated finish. This type of flooring is also best suited to workplaces like offices or libraries along with container homes. It has different shades to offer, and you can choose any of the three depending upon the color selection of your home. It can be a light-colored finish, a medium-colored finish, 0r a dark touch finish. All shades offer the same aesthetic beauty and attraction. The only limitation is that you have to select light mode if you have light theme paint in your home. Prepared with high technology and advanced engineering processes, these floors are durable and robust, and they also resist scratches. You can maintain this flooring easily without any inconvenience.

Pros

1. It is adjustable.
2. It is available in a variety of colors.
3. There are different types and varieties available.
4. It is water-resistant.
5. It is scratch-resistant.
6. It is easily maintainable.
7. It has aesthetic flooring.
8. It is highly durable.
9. It is budget-friendly.
10. It is easily installable.

Cons

1. It is not an eco-friendly flooring.
2. It is non-recyclable and non-decomposable.
3. It can't be repaired.

CHAPTER 14:

Choosing Your
Home's Top Priority

The three things that you need to consider before creating your shipping container home are:

- A design that reflects your taste

- The budget within which your container home will be built

- The timeline

The three marks below are always important, but usually, only 1–2 stand out as being your top priorities for a build. Now you must think about it. Are you looking for an elegant design with a low budget? If you are tired of paying a huge amount to your landlord and want to build your container home as soon as possible then you must follow these simple steps, and if you believe in sustainability then you must build this shipping container home.

As mentioned earlier, deciding on a budget is the most important thing, but now it is time to move forward. Here is a list of other things that you need to do after you have decided on the budget.

Estimate the Square Feet

You must have an idea of the square feet of your home, but if you don't know, then here are some guidelines to help you:

Two Containers

You must use eight 8' by 40' high cube containers every 320 square feet. If you are planning to make a single bedroom and single bathroom home, then you only need two containers. Working with two containers will not only be cost-effective, but it will also take less space and thus will be easy to maintain.

Three Containers

However, everyone has their taste. If you want to have a slightly bigger home, then you must consider having three containers. With three containers, you can easily have two bedrooms. We must have an extra bedroom for when guests visit us, right?

Four Containers

If you are a family with children then you need an even bigger place, and families looking for a three to four-bedroom home must have four containers. These four containers will be sufficient for making three bedrooms and other necessary areas of the house.

Additional Containers

Lastly, if you have a spacious hall in mind or a swimming area or anything else of a similar size then you need even more containers. Having six to seven containers will give you the house of your dreams with extra space to make whatever you want to make in your container home.

CHAPTER 15:

What to Look Out for When Installing Various Utilities and Services

There is a good chance that the basic utilities that you will need for your home are already in place under the street in front of your building site if you are building near a city, larger town, or residential subdivision. During the installation of large utility lines, each building site is served by a smaller branch or "lateral" line, which stays unused until a home is built. Then it is extended and connected to your house, thus providing all of the services the municipality offers.

By burying utilities underground, they are protected from weather and damage. The devices are also unsightly and can cause damage to your health if they are tampered with. Most utilities charge monthly fees based on how much a homeowner uses each service in addition to the initial connection fee. The services provided by a municipality usually include the following:

Water

In the process of installing utilities, a valve called a curb-stop is installed underground at the end of the water lateral. An underground water line runs from your curb-stop to your house during construction, supplying it with water. Curb-stop valves let plumbers cut off municipal water supplies at your residence if needed.

Sewer Pipe

A sewer pipe can be found running from your home to the street where it connects with the municipal sewer system. Sinks, showers, clothes washers, toilets, and dishwashers drain wastewater into sewer mains and into a wastewater treatment plant. Because sewer pipes are laid at a slight pitch, gravity carries all the wastewater to the municipal wastewater treatment plant.

Electricity

Utility companies use above-ground switches called pad-mount transformers to protect high-voltage electrical lines from damage. These switches are always locked. From the power plant to your house, the electric company is in charge of supplying electricity. Electrical installation work during home construction is handled by a licensed electrician.

Gas

Natural gas is mainly supplied to homeowners by pressurized pipes in most municipalities. The connection point between your private gas lateral and the larger gas main is also equipped with a valve similar to a curb-stop on a water line. When needed, or in an emergency, you will be able to shut the gas off.

Phone and Cable

The telephone and cable television lines to your home were once installed by the telephone company. Your phone service would have been connected to the cable company's cable box, while your television would have been connected to your phone service. These fields have seen incredible technological advancements and continue to do so at a rapid pace. The current state of these communications services makes it difficult to give an accurate example.

Smartphones have made landlines obsolete for most homeowners. Satellites and wireless technology are continually changing how we watch television and use computers. You should contact professionals in these areas as you plan your home building project to ensure that your home is constructed with the latest infrastructure. When it comes to easy access to municipal utilities, building near a developed area is advantageous. The builder, as part of his or her building process, will take care of all the necessary connection arrangements.

CHAPTER 16:

Heat Transfer in Shipping Container Homes

Transferring heat into and out of your shipping container home is one of the most energy-consuming processes. The heat can be purposefully moved at times, and it can also be deliberately slowed down at times. When you design and construct a shipping container home or building, you must consider both cases. What is the feeling of touching a hot stove, using a hairdryer, or putting your hand on a bonfire on a cold night during the winter? Thus, you are intuitively aware of heat transfer. My discussion will revolve around the principles of heat transfer and their significance to building container homes. It is important to understand how heat transfer works, even though it is a bit technical. Heating and cooling your container home affects a variety of decisions, including those that may cost you thousands of dollars. To help you navigate these important decisions, I have cut through the irrelevant details to provide examples.

What Is Heat?

Heat transfer can be understood only once you understand how heat itself works. Thermodynamics refers to the change in temperature as heat. If there is no outside force acting on it (like an air conditioner), it will flow from the hotter to the cooler object. It is important to understand that you can add coldness or remove heat to something, but not both. As a result, cold denotes a lack of heat. Air conditioners do not add coolness to your home, they take heat from your home and move it outside (even though it's hotter outside than inside). It is similar to the phenomenon of darkness. A room cannot be darkened; light can only be dimmed.

Types of Heat Transfer

There are three ways in which heat energy can be transferred, each of which is crucial to understanding the context of shipping container structures.

Conduction

In an object with direct contact, heat moves by conduction as it moves within the solid. Heat is transferred from a hot stove to your hand when you touch it. You will eventually get hot if you touch a metal spoon on the burner while holding it in your hand because heat conducts through metal. The heat energy will pass to your hand much less when wearing an oven mitt (insulation). As it is closest to the outside environment, the corrugated metal of a container is usually the hottest (during the summer) or the coldest (during the winter) part of the building. In addition to the insulation, wall studs, window, door frames, etc., everything that touches this external layer of metal will also receive the heat transmitted via conduction. When it comes to conducting, thermal bridges play an important role.

Thermal Bridging

A thermal bridge occurs when a wall section has higher conductivity (or lower insulative capacity) than its surroundings. The conductive heat flow is thus directed down the path of least resistance. Overall, the wall system thus has a lower insulative capacity. The wall studs will conduct heat from the metal exterior directly into the wall studs if they are directly connected to the metal inside the container. Wood, on the other hand, acts much less effectively as a conductor, so the same thing happens with wood studs. As a result, heating will transfer less easily into the interior of the building. The corrugated metal of the container could be placed between the metal wall studs and insulating material. This is an excellent source of information about the insulation properties of common building materials.

Your container should be as separate from its exterior metal as possible. Your aim should be to insulate the interior living space. You will need to place the insulation between the inside wall and the outside corrugated metal to get its full effect. When thermally "bridged" through or around your insulation, this reduces the effectiveness, and you should do everything you can to minimize it as much as possible. Insulation is essentially worthless if it is thermally "bridged". Studs that extend into the container's metal exterior can provide a path for heat to condense right through the insulation to the drywall inside by creating a thermal bridge

Convection

Heat is transferred by convection between solids and fluids, as well as between solids and gases. As an engineering term, fluid describes gases as well as liquids (such as water). Only a slight difference separates the two types of convection.

Natural Convection

The presence of a fluid in a hot object naturally causes it to heat up. A convection current will generally move hot fluid away from a hot object as a result of density changes (and therefore buoyancy) due to increasing temperatures. This is where the expression "heat rises" comes from. You've probably experienced natural convection when you were holding your hand directly above a stove burner and noticed that the air was warmer than elsewhere in the room.

Forced Convection

By using a fan or pump, fluid is sprayed over a hot object. When you use a hairdryer, an electric fan forces air over an electric heating element, which is an example of forced convection.

Convection Taking Place in Shipping Containers

Natural convection increases the temperature of the air surrounding your container roof in the summer (we'll discuss later why the roof becomes hot). Warm air from inside the container rises above the container, where it is constantly exchanged with slightly cooler air in the atmosphere. The placement of ridge vents on top of peaked roofs (and eaves vents on the bottom) allows hot air to escape from the attic through natural convection. Without the proper ventilation, the temperature in your attic rises above the ambient temperature outside of your house.

Nevertheless, container homes don't lend themselves well to this type of design. It is impossible to build an attic in a container home unless you add a peaked roof above the container.

Radiation

Heat transfer via radiation is the last and most difficult to understand of the three modes. Let us first understand how radiation at a high level is different from normal radiation. Radiation at a high level is usually referred to as a very negative thing. Following that, we'll explore what kinds of radiation there are. Radiation refers to the transfer of energy through matter using invisible waves. The two types of radiation can be distinguished in the following way:

Ionizing Radiation

Radiation can cause tissue damage and is the 'bad' radiation you hear about. That's why you wear a lead vest when you have X-rays, and why Chernobyl's accident site is inaccessible to humans.

Non-Ionizing Radiation

There is also a wide range of other electromagnetic radiation. Light and radio waves are among the many types of electromagnetic radiation. We're talking about non-ionizing radiation here, which is thermal radiation.

Thermal Radiation: The Way It Affects Us

This article will not discuss the reasons why most thermal radiation we encounter in the course of normal interaction with the environment occurs in the visible and infrared portions of the spectrum. In cold weather, you may have felt warm standing around a bonfire. This is a good example of thermal radiation. The wood was emitting thermal energy, which was absorbed by your body, increasing your skin's temperature. Another option is to use a thermal camera that can detect the emission of thermal radiation from various objects. Thermodynamically, everything above absolute zero (-273.15°C or -459.67°F) emits thermal radiation.

As a result of your body's temperature rising, you are radiating heat into the room around you right now (this is in addition to the heat conduction coming from the chair you are sitting in and the heat convection that is spreading throughout the room). Both you and the cold water in a room radiate heat energy towards one another. The water in the pool is much cooler than your body, so you send out much more energy than it does. Your body temperature decreases because you're emitting a lot of heat energy but receiving little in return. Having received a lot of thermal radiation from you, the water is not emitting much thermal radiation itself, so it's getting warmer. It would only take a certain amount of time before you would both reach equilibrium.

Thermal Radiation in Shipping Containers

Shipment container homes are mainly heated by solar radiation. There is a wide range of frequencies that the sun emits. Our atmosphere blocks much of it. Among the remaining frequencies is thermal energy. In the hot sun, corrugated metal in a container is heated by convection under the ambient air. Thermal radiation is responsible, however, for causing the temperature of the metal to rise above the ambient air temperature when sunlight hits this outside metal of the container. Using the studs, insulation, and other wall components, the increased heat energy is then transmitted directly into the container by conduction. Conduction cannot be eliminated, but it can be reduced by using materials with low conductivity (and high insulation), as discussed in the section on conduction. The best way to minimize heat gain from thermal radiation is not to insulate against it like with conduction and convection, but to block it (for example, with shade) or reflect it (with reflective coatings or materials) back into the atmosphere.

Cooling Using Thermal Radiation

It's important to remember that thermal radiation doesn't only result in hotter containers. Your container, as well as everything above absolute zero, radiates heat. The container emits energy night and day, just as it does during the day. Since the sun isn't shining anymore, the container is getting much less heat. It is possible for a container to radiate more energy out than it is receiving, which is known as passive radiative cooling or sky cooling, under certain conditions (direct line of sight from the container to the sky with a clear sky free of clouds, etc.). Until the conditions are met, the container can reach temperatures below the ambient temperature. Recent research has focused on special materials that are both excellent at reflecting thermal radiation and emitting their heat. In experiments, materials have been brought down to ambient temperatures when exposed to direct sunlight. The use of special coatings to reduce cooling loads and heat loads could be possible one day with more research and refinement.

Shipping Container Homes and Heat Transfer

Your shipping container home should be a comfortable space whether you live in the city or the country. The appearance is important, but it is equally important to consider the temperature. There will be times when you need to think about heating and cooling your container home unless you live in an extremely mild climate where the use of air conditioners and heaters is not a necessity. You're fighting a battle against physics as well as mother nature whenever you attempt to create a different temperature inside of your container from the outside. You can apply your effort and resources to areas that will have the greatest impact by understanding the principles behind heat transfer. Keeping out the ambient temperature of the air with an insulated bottom can help in a hot environment. It is, however, much more crucial to insulate the top and sides of your container where the sun will be able to radiate heat.

Cool Roof Coating

There are several similarities between cool roof coatings and paint. You can typically apply them in the same way with a roller, brush, or spray rig (depending on the product type). As liquids, they come in containers similar to what is used to purchase paint. Once applied, they look similar. Paint and cool roof coatings are different in several important ways. However, cool roof coatings are designed primarily for thermal performance rather than aesthetics. It is much thicker than conventional aluminum and more able to withstand natural and manmade wear and tear. The pigments in the material reflect and emit specific wavelengths of electromagnetic (particularly thermal) radiation.

Cool Roof Coatings: How Do They Work?

Cool roof coatings are like insulation in that they don't require any additional energy to operate, as opposed to an active system like air conditioning, which utilizes electricity to function. Being more eco-friendly and saving more money is possible by maximizing your passive cooling. Solar radiation is the sun's energy that comes in several wavelengths. Some of these wavelengths correspond to light, others to heat, and others to other things. Roofing coatings designed for cool roofs transmit thermal energy, which we'll call wavelengths that carry heat. There is little attention paid to the effects of these coatings on other types of radiation (like visible light, radio waves, etc.) since the coatings are designed to be able to reflect and emit thermal energy.

Reflected Radiation

As long as your container is facing the sun, it will receive some reflected radiation from other objects as well as from the sun. There is a performance measure for a cool roof coating called 'reflectivity'. Heat can be reflected out when energy is inbound, kind of like a mirror. Most of the benefits of having a cool roof are due to its enhanced reflectivity.

Emitted Radiation

A part of the radiation that is emitted into your container is inbound emitted radiation from all the objects around you. Radiation emitted outward is measured by a cool roof coating performance measure called 'emissivity'. The degree of thermal energy that is re-emitted, or emitted out of the environment, tells us how much thermal energy is internally absorbed. Imagine that you were in a dark room and were sitting across from a warm box; if the box were black instead of white, you would feel more of its heat radiating towards you because black objects tend to have a higher emissivity than white objects.

When to Not Use Cool Roof Coatings

Since white or light-colored roofs are typically in good condition, any small benefits from a cool roof coating probably wouldn't be worth the time and effort it takes to add one. However, cool roof coatings might be a good option for anyone with a darker roof, or a dirty, peeling roof. A cool roof coating is not recommended if you live in an area where it is mostly cold throughout the year. Rather than relying on additional heat sources (like heaters, stoves, etc.) to keep you warm, you'll want to make your containers as heat-absorbing as possible. Cool roof coatings, on the other hand, can have some other positive effects on your heating bill as well. Winter is characterized by lower sun angles than summer, so the sun has less radiant energy. As a result, your container's roof will receive more direct sunlight rather than sunlight coming from above. Also, in snowy climates, your roof coating will be rendered inoperative since the snow will cover your roof.

Cool Roof Coating on the Side Walls of Container Homes

Using a cool roof coating on the walls may also make a measurable difference based on your latitude and how much shade your container home gets throughout the day. Regardless, benefits (if there are any) vary from home to home and from site to site. The impact will increase the more direct sunlight it receives and the closer it is to a 90-degree angle of incidence. It is important to consider aesthetics regardless of potential benefits. In general, coatings on walls will be more noticeable than coatings on roofs. Consequently, you may be able to paint the walls white, but the roof will probably need to be painted. There are also many colors available for cool coatings, but be sure you have the right amount of exposure to the sun before paying a premium price for one.

White Paint Instead of Cool Roof Coating

A cool roof coating does not necessarily have to be white. The fact that they work with light outside the visible spectrum, and that they use special pigments, allows cool roofs to be many different colors. Nevertheless, if all other things are equal, lighter colors perform better. White paint also reflects light, so that needs to be considered. The reflections created by windows on the 2nd and 3rd floors of multilevel houses and nearby multilevel buildings can be quite problematic at certain times of the day, especially if you live in a multilevel neighborhood. Some of the performance benefits of cool roof coatings can be gained without the reflections that get in the way.

Finally, regular paint will not hold up to the weather as well as a cool roof coating, so it's important to keep that in mind. It is usually better to use a thick, durable coating on roofs because they are subject to extreme conditions and harsh weather conditions. Furthermore, it isn't something you want to do quite as often as you have to climb up on your roof to paint (or pay someone to do so for you). If you are preparing to build or upgrade a container home, the cool roof coating is an option that you may want to consider. It's easy to lower the exterior temperature of your container with just a little bit of money and a few hours of work. Your geographic location, home design, insulation level, and other factors can affect how much you save on your utility bills.

CHAPTER 17:

Condensation in Shipping Container Homes

Condensation is the worst thing that can happen to a container home. It's most prevalent on the top six inches on the interior wall of the container roof. While building your container home, you have to make sure that your container walls do not condense. This mainly occurs due to the dramatic changes in the weather when the temperature falls. With the drop in temperature, the humidity level increases, which is called 'the dew point'. The water vapors form and condense; these vapors are known as 'container rain'. They then adhere to the walls of the container in liquid form, thus contributing to condensation.

Reasons for Condensation

Before moving on to the solutions, it is crucial to have a look at the reasons that might cause condensation in container homes.

Temperature

When the climate or temperature inside the containers is humid, then there can be a concentration of moisture that makes the air condense. It can be caused by excess use of water inside of the home, which makes the water vaporize and condense at a low temperature. This can be very damaging for the container walls and also the interior design of your home. Other than that, there can be two different temperature conditions of both inner and outer environments in which condensation can occur in shipping container homes.

Cold External Environment and Interior Heating

One of the properties of steel containers is that they are affected by the change in the temperature easily and adapt to that temperature. So, when the outer temperature is low and cold and the interior heating is producing a high temperature, there will be low moisture inside. But slowly, due to the low temperature outside, the inner environment can pick up the water vapors quickly. It can be due to diffusion or infiltration, thus increasing the condensation effect in the interior home as well.

Warm External Environment and Interior Cooling

When the temperature of the outer environment is warm and humid, you try to keep the inner temperature cool to protect yourself from the heat. In this way, the coolness inside can lead to an increase in moisture if the cooling system is left running for too long. There are also many other ways, such as air entering due to open windows, improperly sealed penetrations, and extremely cool temperatures of the inner area. If you use the air conditioner inside your home, it might be possible that the air inside the evaporator coil of the air conditioner condenses.

Hygroscopic Materials

Hygroscopic products are those that contain moisture in them. These can be the moisture-containing materials that are used in the home. These can be the following:

Showers

The shower is an essential material used in bathrooms. In winter, when you use a warm water shower, it might be possible that air becomes saturated. This leads to the formation of water vapors. If there is proper ventilation, then this can be avoided. But with improper ventilation, it stays inside and forms condensation.

Dish Washers

If water remains for a prolonged time in the dish washer, then it can also be a source of moisture. Or, if the dishwasher is kept open after the cleaning cycle, you can easily create humidity in your kitchen.

Wet Clothes

If you keep your washed clothes inside your home to dry, there is a good chance of keeping the water vapors locked inside.

Ironing Clothes

A steam iron usually involves increases in steam and water vapors, so it is no surprise that it can lead to condensation as well.

Damp Building Materials

While building a container home or setting the grass of your garden, you may use materials that are damp – this can also lead to condensation.

Non-Electric Space Heaters

Through combustion, heating devices like gas and oil-fired heaters dispose of moisture. If they're ventilated, then there are fewer chances of condensation.

Improper Ventilation

Obstruction of the air inside the container will let all the airdrops inside by the time that condensations forms and clings to the walls of the container. Therefore, improper ventilation often becomes a cause of the unequal maintenance of temperature inside the home, which then leads to less air movement inside and outside of the home. Ultimately, this increases condensation.

Air Space

Though ventilation is necessary, it doesn't mean there will be excess air space in the home compared to the outside. Ventilation creates a balance between outer and inner environmental temperatures, while the air space increases the passage of entry of the vapors inside the home. The more air space there is, the more moisture and condensation there will be.

Container Usage

Using containers during the building process is a crucial factor to consider when thinking of the causes of condensation. You can consider how the containers were packed and transferred – what time of day it was and for how long they were unpacked and left open.

Perspiration

Perspiration occurs in the summer season when the temperature of the body cools down. This causes sweating and water vapors to move in the interior air. If there's no ventilation, they condense.

Respiration

Respiration is a constant process; you inhale and exhale. In winter, you may have noticed that you inhale air but in the process of exhalation, your breath turns foggy. This air contains a lot of moisture in its condensed form. When this is attached to the walls of the container, it forms a layer. When left for many hours without ventilation, it causes corrosion in the container walls.

How to Avoid Condensation in a Container Home

Condensation in containers homes mainly occurs due to moisture. The excess moisture can lead to corrosion and mold formation in containers, ultimately ruining your container home. So, it's necessary to control the moisture in the container. You can do so by keeping the container dry as much as you can. There are also many other ways to avoid or reduce the condensation in a container home. For all of the above reasons, given below are the perfect ways to eliminate condensation. Following these simple tips will help to keep your home moisture-free.

Insulation

Insulation is the most effective way to protect the containers from getting corroded. It's even better than cladding the interior of the container. Insulation in the walls of the container, both inside and outside, can effectively reduce the amount of water vapor getting into the home. It helps to maintain the optimum warm temperature that is below the dew point. Hence, the temperature differences between inner and outer environments will not become significant. You can choose any insulation discussed before in this book – all types of insulation are good at reducing condensation. It all depends on your own preferences, as well as your budget. There are also other ways, such as using bubble wrap foil, polystyrene insulation, or aluminum barriers.

Ventilation

Ventilation serves a great purpose for maintaining a balance between the temperature of the outside atmosphere and the inside environment. They'll become equal, and there'll be no effect for condensation. Another benefit of this is that the moist, humid air is drawn outside the container through ventilation while allowing the air inside with ambient temperature. In this way, the water content in the air is significantly reduced. There are many ways to ventilate your container home – using small vents for ventilation, large steel louvered vents, or turbine/whirlybird vents. Other than these, grate-style vents can also be a good option for ventilation. In addition, you also have to consider another factor: what is the outside temperature of the place where you live. Sometimes, installing ventilation in the most humid places or having a humid temperature throughout the year can be the wrong choice.

Desiccants

Desiccants are substances that help to maintain the dryness level inside your container home by reducing the moisture. They are good for reducing or preventing container rain. There are a variety of desiccants available – calcium sulfate, silica, calcium chloride, charcoal, etc. You can use any for this purpose. They all work the same way to maintain the ambient temperature. Although they are all effective in reducing condensation, the usage matters, so make sure you use an adequate amount! After using them, keep an eye out to check if the required amount is working well or not. You can use these in dry bags and put them on the floor, you can use them in paint and apply them to container walls, or you can use them in poles that are used on the container walls. Have a good look at the different types of desiccants to get a better idea of what you should buy and use.

Desiccant Blankets

Desiccant blankets are like membranes hung above the containers or goods in the container home. The membranous feature absorbs all of the container rain and is sealed in this way to reduce condensation. They have a leak-proof design that moves the moisture from goods upward without letting it drain down into the home. This protects both the hoods available in the home and also the container from the condensation of the water droplets.

Desiccant Pads

These pads are placed below products like beverages and other things that contain moisture. When drinks and moist foods are placed on these pads, the water is sucked in and condensation is reduced. They also protect food from fungus growth. Some pads also offer thermal protection, too.

Desiccant Bags

Desiccant bags are used for the same purpose as desiccant pads. They absorb the water content thus reducing the humidity outside. You can put moist food or materials into desiccant bags and also pack goods and food in them so that there is no leakage of water outside of the bags into the interior atmosphere of the home. Thus, the dew temperature is reduced and doesn't allow water vapors to move outside.

Dehumidifier

The term 'dehumidifier' indicates that these devices are used to remove humidity. On average, if you buy a good humidifier and place it in your home, it can keep humidity below 40%. You can choose a small dehumidifier for $200 if you are trying to keep the cost low, but if you can afford to invest the money then it is best to install a large dehumidifier for $300. If you want to keep it working well to reduce humidity, it's necessary to remove the water regularly. Alternatively, you can install a hose into it that can drain water and reduce moisture content that has been collected due to water storage.

Pallets

The use of pallets is common for the storage of goods in shipping container homes, but the use of the right pallets in container homes is very crucial because it affects the amount of moisture in the home. If you use wooden pallets that are made from freshly cut wood, then they should be able to absorb the most moisture (these types of pallets are estimated to absorb 35–60% of the moisture). Old pallets are often too heavily affected by moisture, especially if they have been kept in damp or wet environments.

Kitty Litter

Kitty litter, also known as cat litter, is used to reduce condensation. This is not just effective and efficient but is also affordable. Kitty litter absorbs moisture, thus reducing the condensation inside your container home. You can use this anywhere in the home, especially the parts that are the most humid. The simple way to use it is to put it in a bowl with holes or a small container with an open lid, then place it in a room where there is a need to avoid condensation. It is very effective in soaking up moisture, keeping your home water vapor-free.

CHAPTER 18:

Safety Concerns

Besides the benefits of affordability and pleasing aesthetics, container homes also come with a number of safety concerns that must be addressed. When you are buying your first containers, you need to ask yourself whether they are safe for your family to live in. Often, this is not the case. Steel containers are usually treated for chemicals to protect them from damage and the effects of aging and corrosion. With this in mind, if you want to live in a container home, you must think ahead about these things and make sure that your containers are safe to live in. Making your container home chemical-free is the first step. This will be discussed below, along with other safety considerations that you must keep in mind before moving into your container home.

Reasons for Toxicity in Container Homes

There are two main sources of toxicity and chemicals in container homes:

Wooden Floors

The first cause is wooded flooring. We know that wood is very prone to dampness and moisture. If wooded flooring is heavily affected by moisture, this can lead to fungus, ultimately ruining the flooring of the container home. For this reason, they are treated with chemicals. These chemicals can be harmful in the long run and are not good for a family to live around every day.

Toxic Paint

Some paints are composed of toxic chemicals like phosphorus or chromates. When the walls are coated with such toxic materials, then the environment is harmful to breathe in. Physical contact with such layering may become problematic because it can affect you when you come into contact with it directly. The coatings of second-hand containers might potentially contain chemicals toxic to humans at certain levels. Containers are coated with these materials to protect them from extreme elements, including direct sunlight exposure and saltwater exposure during transit.

Physical contact with the coating is usually more dangerous than off-gassing. It is important to find out which coatings were used to determine potential risks as not all coatings are problematic. To determine exactly what coatings were used, you can try contacting the container manufacturer and finding the MSDS for those coatings. Most people are unable to do this, so they tend to assume the worst as a precaution. Sandblasting is ideal for removing paint by using an abrasive such as sand. In addition to being labor-intensive, it is also hazardous when the coating is being sprayed and removed.

Can Shipping Container Homes Withstand Hurricanes?

A lot of people ask the question of whether or not container homes are hurricane-proof. You need to consider what the shipping container was originally designed to do to answer this question. Shipping containers were designed to transport goods around the world, so they should be airtight and impenetrable.

According to our 'A Complete History of the Shipping Container', after shipping containers were first used in the 1950s, cargo theft and loss declined significantly. Goods were loaded as bulk cargo on ships before shipping containers were invented. This means that the goods were either packed into sacks, barrels, or crates. The goods were stolen by light-handed laborers. Originally, it was called the shipping cost. In contrast, the number of stolen goods drastically declined when shipping containers appeared on the scene. Since shipping containers could be locked by their owners before loading, they could avoid the possibility of theft.

Shipping containers are probably the most secure form of storage you'll find. However, converting containers into houses often results in people removing metal and altering the structure, decreasing the security of the container. Even though shipping containers are not traditional buildings, they can be just as secure as traditional homes, but the original structure of the container must be kept intact if you intend to live in your shipping container at a remote location. The shipping container doors have to be replaced with more traditional windows and doors so that this can be accomplished.

CHAPTER 19:

The Detoxification of
Shipping Container Homes

I f you are thinking of using old containers for building a home, you have to consider other factors like the use of chemicals. It is possible that chemicals were used to keep them in a good position or to protect them from further damage while shipping. Other than the walls, their floors are also sealed with chemicals to prevent corrosion. This is harmful if you are going to live in that container. In this regard, you have to do some procedures that can help remove the toxic chemicals from the container home. We are going to discuss three ways you chemically remediate your container home.

Encapsulation with Paint

Encapsulation is essentially covering the coating with something else. Asbestos and lead-based paint are common commercial remediation techniques that involve encapsulation. If you are concerned about the coatings on shipping containers, I recommend encapsulation. To ensure that any encapsulation products you intend to use will bond properly, consult the manufacturer. Encapsulation involves covering the questionable surface with another surface so that you will no longer be prone to touching it. Because the coating underneath isn't disturbed, it's quicker, easier, and cheaper than other methods. The best way to cover the eroded part and also to decrease the damage of chemicals and pests is to paint the container home from both the inside and outside. You have to paint all the roofs, rooms, and places where you know the chemicals or pests are used. Here we will tell you how you can do this:

1. Firstly, use a rug and remove any bumps in the corroded part.
2. Then, take a power washer and clean it completely from the inside of the shipping container.
3. Wash it with water and let all the containers dry. This will take time; for a faster drying time, allow some air to come inside (you can do this by opening the ventilators).
4. Once they are dry, put the primer first on the walls of the container. Primer is necessary as it sets the base first.
5. Now use a sprayer and fill it with the paint.
6. Apply it by opening the nozzle a little, making sure to cover all the areas. Cover the marks and the parts affected by chemicals in paint.

It is recommended that you buy toxic chemical-free paint for the interior of your home as it is eco-friendly.

Replacing the Existing Flooring with Eco-Friendly Flooring

If you find your old flooring toxic or abundant in chemicals, then you can opt for another option. This is a little costly and requires more work, but it will be good for you and other people living inside the home. Many floorings are eco-friendly. If the old flooring has been damaged by pests or water, then wait no further and replace it with a new one and fill the part where there are holes (wood that is filled with excessive moisture can be a breeding ground for toxicity and fungus and can cause harm).

Follow this procedure to remove and replace the existing wood flooring:

1. Thoroughly check the parts of the wood flooring that are damaged.

2. Make sure to take the exact dimensions inside the container home and buy lumber accordingly.

3. Through the use of a saw, cut the old wood flooring and remove it.

4. Consider using a long pry bar as they are sturdy and can help to remove the large and small pieces easily.

5. After removal of the old wood, put in the new pieces and fix them into place.

Encapsulating the Existing Flooring

If you find that it is too much work to remove and fix the new flooring, another alternative is to encapsulate the old one with a new layer of flooring. Encapsulation has the same effect as covering the wood flooring. Hence, there will be no harm from the chemicals that were used in the wooden flooring. You can use marine plywood for this purpose as it is not toxic or harmful. The dimensions of marine plywood are 4' × 8'. To guarantee a safe environment, buy ceramic tiles and cover the underlayment with them.

1. Measure the area or the tiles of wood that are damaged and toxic.

2. Buy the marine plywood, taking into consideration the dimensions of the damaged part of the wood.

3. Cut the plywood with the use of a saw into the exact pieces where they are needed.

4. An adhesive is needed for attachment purposes. Make sure that it is not toxic.

5. Apply the adhesive to the downward side of the plywood.

6. Place or paste it onto the damaged parts you want to cover (you can even use it for your whole home).

7. Place a plastic spacer on the edges of the tiles.

8. When all the tiles are attached, apply grout at the edges.

9. Remove the excess grout using a dampened sponge.

It will take some time to set up. Make sure to not disturb the tiles during the setting process.

CHAPTER 20:

How to Make Shipping Container Homes Environment Friendly

You might have heard that container homes are eco-friendly, but not all are. You can understand this better by considering the time that Philip Clark filed a patent to use shipping containers and construct a home out of them. This was not seen as a good idea at the time, but now, everything from homes to coffee houses can be made into green, environment-friendly spaces by using shipping containers, so there is no excuse for not making an effort to make your home environmentally friendly.

Here are some recommendations and tips that will help you on your way to making your house eco-friendly and green:

Use Eco-friendly Insulation

Using eco-friendly insulation is important, especially if you are deciding to make the move to a container home for environmental reasons. Insulation will also help you to maintain the temperature of your home, avoid mold and fungus, and keep your energy bills low. You need to consider two things: what to use as an insulator for your home and where to install it in your home. Factors such as climate and environment will have an impact on these decisions. You should also consider the possibility of condensation.

Here are the materials that you can use to insulate the containers:

Strawbale

Straw bale is made from the residue of barley, rice, and wheat. Strawbale insulation has a thickness of 18–24 inches. It depends on how thick you want your insulation to be, as well as the height of the walls. There are several benefits to using this type of insulation:

- Combat climate change
- Affordable
- Excellent insulation properties
- Renewable properties
- Easily sourced
- Customizable and easy to fix into place

Hempcrete

Hempcrete is a great moisture-handling material that is perfect for insulation. It provides the following benefits:

- Reasonably affordable
- Non-toxic insulation material
- Maintains integrity

- Handles resistance
- Good structural quality
- Agricultural by-product

Blanket Insulation

Yes, you read that right! Blankets (the kind that you use to keep warm at night) are excellent for insulation, especially in container homes. Insulation blankets can be made of rockwool, sheep's wool, cotton, slag wool, mineral wool, and a variety of other materials. Whatever you choose to use, it is a cheap method and is starting to trend in western countries. How can you use blankets as insulation? Take the material fibers, fit them into a cavity studded in between and fix them to support internal walls.

Spray Insulation

This is applied by spraying the liquid material on the containers, which later solidifies and becomes an insulated sheet above and in between the cavities. It is good for both summer and winter as the solid material fills all the gaps, so there is no exchange of heat or cold. There are many types of spray insulation available, including:

- Damp spray cellulose insulation
- Closed-cell spray polyurethane foam
- Open-cell spray polyurethane foam
- Non-expanding sprayed-in insulation

Expanded Foam Insulation

Expanded foam insulation is applied to boards and panels that are manufactured offsite. These are self-supporting boards of different sizes. Moreover, they can be customized on-site according to the required size for windows, doors, or roofs. Expanded foam insulation is DIY-friendly and can be attached to the wall of the container without hassle.

Reflective Barriers

Barriers are mostly used where you get a lot of radiation or you live in a climate that is very hot. Reflective barriers reflect heat radiation away from your home and are one of the most effective forms of insulation for this reason. They are specially designed barriers with a coating that becomes a barrier for all types of radiation, including heat and harmful ultraviolet radiation. Hence, the interior of your house will be cool, safe, and radiation-free.

Loose-Fill Insulation

Loose-fill insulation is just like the cavity filling of a tooth. The container walls have cavities, so this insulation is applied by filling these cavities with materials by the use of a machine. These machines use macroscopic insulation materials like perlite, vermiculite, and fiberglass. This is an eco-friendly option to choose for container home insulation and is also cost-effective, but it will give you one disadvantage: it cannot withstand poor weather conditions because of its water permeability.

Denim Insulation

When thinking of the best insulator and noise absorber, denim is the best choice you can opt for. To make the place more environmentally friendly, safe, and comfortable to live in, you should go for denim insulation for the walls of your containers. Not only does denim do a great job of absorbing moisture, but it is also great for noise pollution too. It is also a fungi-resistant material. However, it is more costly than fiberglass.

Cork Insulation

Using cork as an insulator is also a great choice. It is eco-friendly, affordable, renewable, and biodegradable. Moreover, cork insulation will provide you with acoustic effects. It acts as an acoustic buffer by producing a sound between the walls and its layer.

Rooftop Garden

Creating a rooftop garden not just becomes a source of insulation but also refreshes your home environment and offers a place to refresh yourself. The soil and the grass will become a source of insulation, reducing the global warming effect on your house by reducing the solar radiation intake. In addition, just imagine how cool and relaxing it will be to lie under the sun or stars in your rooftop garden!

Keep Your Garden Green

Keeping your garden green will make your house green by providing you with fresh air to breathe in the container home. Also, there should be no wastage of containers. You can recycle them or put them into use by turning them into pots for grafting small plants. Moreover, waste food, or organic waste, is something you can use to throw into the garden as it will become a source of fertilizer for grass and other plants. The other benefit is that you can grow vegetables easily.

Maintain the Temperature

Maintaining the temperature in any season is necessary to keep a healthy environment inside your container home. Otherwise, in summer, you will feel like the sun is directly above you and in winter, you will feel like a snowman. So, what should you do in both cases?

The best solution for keeping it cool in the summers is to paint the walls or use box fans. Another way is to install a window AC unit, but this may be costly. It all depends on your budget and your personal priorities. As for winter, it is recommended that you insulate the walls or use space heaters or wood-burning stoves to keep it warm inside.

Smart Use of Appliances

It's time to be smart! Keep an eye on the devices and appliances you always leave on standby mode. Think about it for a second – are they using electricity? If so, turn them off when they're not in use and save your money from now on by aiming to shut down all the electrical appliances after use. This will not only reduce the electricity bills but also reduce your carbon footprint, which is crucial for an eco-friendly environment at home.

Install Photovoltaic Solar Panels

You may have already spent a lot of money while building your container home, so why not keep more in your pockets from here onwards? Installing photovoltaic solar panels will not only save your money wasted on energy but will also help to reduce your carbon footprint and benefit the broader environment in all kinds of ways. Using photovoltaic solar panels is great if you want to live off-grid or if you just want a backup when electricity is down in your area. Just make sure to put them someplace where they are facing the sunlight directly.

Use Energy-efficient Light Bulbs

Even after installing the solar panel system, the need for light bulbs is irreplaceable. It is very difficult to replace light bulbs as they are an ideal source of light. However, it is possible to use power-saving light bulbs instead of power-consuming incandescent bulbs. This is now made possible with the advancement of LED light bulbs. LED light bulbs have been growing in popularity in recent years. You can now get the bonus advantage of low-cost LED bulbs with an 85% power saving.

Use Locally Sourced Materials

Using local building materials for container home construction is very advantageous if you want to save money. However, it is not always easy to get hold of the right supplies and materials; it really depends on where you are located. For instance, if you are living in Canada, you can easily find oak for insulating container walls, but if you're looking for oak in Dubai, you are going to struggle. If you do find some good quality locally sourced material, make sure you use it to good effect. Different materials are better suited to different uses and environments, so when using locally sourced materials, make sure you are using them right.

Use Eco-Friendly Home Accessories

What do I mean by eco-friendly accessories? I am referring to the use of tools, equipment, and accessories that support a healthy and fresh environment inside the home.

- Use water-efficient showerheads in the kitchen and washrooms
- Use eco-friendly electric equipment like kettles, boilers, and geysers
- Use carpets to keep your home warm in the winter
- Use wool bed sheets and comforters
- Make sure that your fridge and other electrical equipment are kept in the shade and out of sunlight

Drain Rainwater Properly

A proper drainage system is essential no matter what kind of home you are building. A good rainwater drainage system should be included in your plan before you even begin to build your home. Nobody wants to live in a home that is prone to leaking and mold the rainwater that falls on it is not distributed appropriately. The proper solution for this is to install a plumbing system in the same way that you would in your brick house. The plumber will drain holes in the floor of the container, passing the pipes through and fixing them so that there is no leakage. Make sure to do this for proper drainage of rainwater from the roof or other parts of the house, along with the kitchen and bathroom plumbing.

Add Shades Above the Roof of Your Container

Adding a shade to your container home is a great way to stop heat from radiating into the container. In short, shades are fixed above the roof of the container home, adding an extra layer of protection and preventing sunbeams from reaching the roof of your home directly. It acts as a filter and is a great way to control the internal temperature of your home and reduce the need for costly AC equipment or the constant use of electric fans. There are several factors to consider when buying a shade for your container home.

- The shade of the container roof should be made of sturdy material so that it can hold solar panels.

- It should cover the whole container or rooftop to stop the sunlight and radiation from entering the home.

- It can be extended slightly to provide additional shade in front of your house.

- It should also have a high pitch so that rainwater can run off easily.

CHAPTER 21:

Important Steps to Remember When Building a Shipping Container Home

~~~

Placing the Containers

By using cranes and delivery trucks, shipping containers can be placed onto foundations relatively easily. An electric crane is easier, faster, and safer than anything else. Renting a rough terrain forklift (or hiring a builder) would be best if you don't own one. A large crowbar can be used to make any final adjustments after your shipping container has been placed on its foundations.

Cutting

A shipping container must be stripped of metal to create the walls that will hold the windows and doors. There are various tools to cut through steel shipping containers, such as plasma cutters, cutting torches, grinders, and even jigsaws (for small openings). A plasma cutter or cutting torch works best when removing an entire wall. You should consult with your structural expert before beginning to cut openings as it is dangerous to remove the structural elements of shipping containers if not done correctly. Starting out with a brand-new container, cut holes for windows, doors, skylights, and accessories. You will need to seal any gaps left to protect the interior from the effects of outside elements.

Adding Doors and Windows

The flooring, windows, and doors need to be added if you want to live in your shipping containers. There are many options for doors and windows, from regular to French style to sliding to cranking. The style you choose should be based on your personal preferences. Consider framing your shipping container's interior with 1 ½-inch steel studs to save as much interior space as possible. Spray foam insulation works well and is very stiff. It might be necessary to use steel studs where the foam hasn't connected the wall and studs. The stud spacing can be narrowed and a layer of drywall can be added. Consider including a thermal break between the metal walls of the shipping container and the studs. A steel stud is particularly effective at transferring heat from the interior to the exterior.

Installing Electric Wires and Plumbing

Unless you are a qualified electrician, you will need to hire a professional to install electric wires in your container home. Even if you think the process looks easy, you don't want to risk the potential accidents or fires that could occur as a result of faulty wiring. The same goes for plumbing – in fact, the two are related as bad plumbing and exposed wiring are an obvious recipe for fire. So, unless you're a qualified plumber or electrician, make sure that you hire a professional for both tasks if you value your safety!

Temperature Control

You'll need insulation to control the temperature inside the home and to keep it cool enough in the summer and warm enough in the winter. Insulating the inside is easier but will mean you sacrificing space. If interior space is a priority for you, then you should invest in external insulation. Not only will this be good for the environment, but it will also be energy efficient and will save you a lot of money in energy bills (you won't have to use expensive AC equipment in the summer or radiators in the winter).

Landscaping

You now have a beautiful shipping container home. Now consider the area around your container. Make sure your home is in harmony with its surroundings by adding a deck or landscape garden. You can even add a roof garden as explained in the previous chapter. Not only does this give you a beautiful place to relax and enjoy the weather and environment, but it also adds a very effective layer of insulation to the roof of your home.

CONCLUSION

In the wake of the increasing creativity of architects and designers, the use of shipping containers is not just confined to shipping products across the seas. Now these containers are serving as the foundation of a new, evergreen living style. The idea of a steel home may seem strange, but yes, a steel home can be an amazing and aesthetically pleasing building with proper planning and design.

Researching before building a home is necessary to figure out how you want your living space to look and what purpose you want it to serve. This is why this guide will come in handy as you will learn everything from where to get the shipping containers to the importance of the soil on which you are building your container home. Home is the safest place, and that is why I have added every little detail to make your shipping container home a haven for you.

Finally, if you feel like you are capable of building a container home yourself, then you must dive into this book to know what kind of equipment you need and what kind of material you should use. the information, be it technical or non-technical, is written in this book in detail. For instance, you can also learn about the pros and cons of cool roofing, so you have a clear and concise idea of what your container home is going to have. Another important thing is that this book has addressed all of the concerns regarding hurricanes and other natural disasters in case you are thinking of building your home in an area where these calamities occur frequently. Go through this book line by line, and you will see that if you started as a person with zero knowledge of shipping containers, you have come out as a person who knows everything that one needs to know before building a shipping container home.

Printed in Great Britain
by Amazon